Theories

Lifespan Development

Mary Hollingsworth

Published by Linus Learning.
Ronkonkoma, NY 11779

ISBN 13: 978-1-60797-686-8
ISBN 10: 1-60797-686-2

Printed in the United States of America.

This book is printed on acid-free paper.

Print Number 5 4 3 2 1

TABLE OF CONTENTS

CHAPTER 3

CHAPTER 4

Introduction

This workbook provides exploration of the most common theories on human development across a lifespan. It is designed to supplement traditional texts on lifespan development through focus on theories of development that can be applied across multiple stages of life, so that students can use this focus as both a foundation of study and a framework of study for development through all the stages of life.

This first chapter provides background on the theories with an outline of workbook contents. Part II provides discussion of the theories organized by focus of development. Part III provides discussion of the areas of development involved in each stage of life. Part IV provides discussion of the lifespan stages with application of the multiple theories to each stage. Part V provides opportunity to blend knowledge and insight into reflections about one's own lifespan development. Part VI facilitates application of this knowledge and insight for personal and professional life. Part VII provides the list of references for the workbook.

Each section and sub-section begins with a chapter to introduce and summarize the contents of that section or subsection. Summarization includes tables to provide an overview of the section or subsection content. Additional exercises and resources are also provided for the focus of the section or subsection.

Each chapter on a theory, area of personal development, or lifespan stage is formatted the same with:

Background – Discussion on the respective theory or lifespan stage.

Exercises – Exercises for students to apply concepts of the chapter in real-life situations.

Case Studies for Lifespan Stages – A case study on an individual for that stage in which cognitive, emotional, moral, physical, and social factors are discussed and the person is discussed in light of the different theories.

Practice Test Items – Practice test questions that can be to review material or for course tests.

Additional Resources – Links for websites, videos, articles, and classroom materials.

Tips for Instructors –Tips for instructor integration in course work on lifespan development.

Tips for Students – Tips for student in integration into course study or life application.

CHAPTER 1

Introduction

Throughout our lives, many influences mold our development into the multifaceted beings that we are. As humans, we each have parts of us that are cognitive, emotional, moral, physical, and social. Some of these influences impact a certain part of us more strongly than others. All of the influences mold the development of all the parts of us into the unique whole person that each of us is.

Several different theories have guided our understanding of human development over a lifespan. Courses and textbooks on development over the lifespan integrate these theories into each stage of development. It can be helpful to students to gain a foundation of understanding about these theories before moving into study of the different stages of development across life.

This workbook provides exploration of the most common theories on human development across a lifespan. It is designed to supplement traditional texts on lifespan development through focus on theories of development that can be applied across multiple stages of life, so that students can use this focus as both a foundation of study and a framework of study for development through all the stages of life.

This workbook is designed to help supplement traditional texts on lifespan development as students build a foundation of understanding the theories and applying what they learn through continuing study of each stage of life. The workbook is not intended for use as a stand-alone text in that traditional textbooks on lifespan development provide significant background detail on theories as integrated within the text chapters and may include mention of additional theories not explored in this workbook. Instead, the workbook presents focus on theories of development that can be applied across multiple stages of life, so that students can use this focus as both a foundation of study and a framework of study for development through all the stages of life.

This first chapter provides background on the theories with an outline of workbook contents. Part II provides discussion of the theories organized by focus of development. Part III provides discussion of the areas of development involved in each stage of life. Part IV provides discussion of the lifespan stages with application of the multiple theories to each stage. Part V provides opportunity to blend knowledge and insight into reflections about one's own lifespan development. Part VI facilitates application of this knowledge and insight for personal and professional life. Part VII provides the list of references for the workbook.

Each section and sub-section begins with a chapter to introduce and summarize the contents of that section or subsection. Summarization includes tables to provide an overview of the section or subsection content. Additional exercises and resources are also provided for the focus of the section or subsection.

Each chapter on a theory, area of personal development, or lifespan stage is formatted the same with:

Background –Discussion on the respective theory or lifespan stage.

Exercises –Exercises for students to apply concepts of the chapter in real-life situations.

Case Studies for Lifespan Stages –A case study on an individual for that stage in which cognitive, emotional, moral, physical, and social factors are discussed and the person is discussed in light of the different theories.

Practice Test Items –Practice test questions that can be to review material or for course tests.

Additional Resources –Links for websites, videos, articles, and classroom materials.

Tips for Instructors –Tips for instructor integration in course work on lifespan development.

Tips for Students –Tips for student in integration into course study or life application.

Theories

Theories are explanations of a phenomenon. This workbook provides exploration of those most commonly presented in course work on human development across a lifespan. Some of the theories cover multiple influences on development and some cover more specific areas of development. The most useful conceptual of development actually includes a blending of theories which gives a complete picture of a person's lifelong development.

Psychoanalytic theories are among the older theories of human development. These focus on the inner and unconscious drives and motives of a person as determining factors in a person's behavior and development. These theories also emphasize the importance of early life experiences as important developmental foundations for later life. The Psychoanalytic theories covered here provide stages of development that have alignment with chronological ages and stages of development.

- **Freud**

  Sigmund Freud's theory provide a foundation for most of the counseling and psychological theories practiced today. He focused on the role of the unconscious in human development. Much of his work explored conflicts that a person experience between their inner drives and life expectations from the world around them. Freud believed that sexual drive was the primary motivation for human behavior. Freud's stages are known as psychosexual stages as Freud believed that the focus of pleasure and sexual impulses shifted over life to different parts of the body – this is reflected in the name of stages in this theory. Later psychoanalytic theorists provided explanation of human development that moved away from Freud's emphasis on sexual instincts. Freud's theory includes stages from birth through puberty. The last stage begins with puberty and lasts for the rest of life.

- **Erikson**

  Erik Erikson built on Freud's theory through a focus on social factors as primary motivation for development. His theory presented certain psychological and social tasks that a person should master at each lifespan stage of development. This theory frames these tasks as crises that are presented – Corey (20xx) explains these also as turning points in life. According to this theory, a person makes a life choice and resolves the crisis to move forward to the next stage with healthy development or does not resolve the crisis and moves forward with some developmental challenges. Erikson's theory provides stages from Infancy through Late Adulthood.

Cognitive theories emphasize the development of thinking and cognitive understanding of the world that a person lives in. Santrock (2015) noted that the cognitive theories emphasize a person's active construction of understanding. As a person makes sense of his world, he takes this understanding and then interacts with his world.

- **Piaget**

  Jean Piaget presented four stages of development through which children cognitively construct their world. Piaget proposed that cognitive development changes over these stages as a child constantly strives to understand his world (Woolfolk and Perry, 2015). This is done as a person gathers information and then organizes that information. Piaget's four stages of development begin with birth and conclude with a developmental stage beginning at age 11 and continuation through adulthood. Piaget's theory also included aspects of moral development.

- **Vygotsky**

  Leo Vygotsky also believed that children actively construct knowledge about their world. He emphasized the roles of social interaction and cultural influence in cognitive development. Vygotsky's theory provided a framework of learning through interaction and influence of their social and cultural worlds. Vygotsky's theory is not organized into specific stages per certain chronological age, but rather provides a framework that could apply to any lifespan stage.

- **Information-Processing Theory**

  This theory focuses on how cognitive development is based on increasing capacity for processing information as a person manipulates information, monitors the information, and creates strategy with the information. Santrock (2015) noted that Robert Siegler was a key figure in creation of this theory and presented thinking as the process of perceiving, encoding, representing, storing, and retrieving information. A core part of cognitive development was learning good strategies for processing information. As with Vygotsky, this theory is not organized into specific stages.

Behavioral Theories focus on human development as observable behavior that reflects what a person is learning. This learning is through experience with the environment. These theories do not present development as sequential stages, but rather development as reflection of the continuity of learning as exhibited in observable behavior.

- **Bandura**

  Albert Bandura emphasized the mutual developmental influences of behavior, the person/cognition, and the environment. A core concept is this approach is observational learning in which a person develops from the influences from what he observes in others and then integrates these observed behaviors into his own life.

- **Skinner**

  B.F. Skinner is known for his work in Operant Conditioning, which is a process of behavioral formation in which the consequences of a behavior will influence the future probability of that behavior's occurrence. Rewards and punishments shape development through the influence of these on behavior. Patterns of behavior frame a person's overall development.

Biological and Contextual Theories expound further on the influences of nature and nurture in human development. These theories elaborate on the role of nature in development as development occurs from a person's organic, genetic inheritance as well as the environmental influences commonly considered to be the nurture side of influence in development.

- **Ethological Theory** focuses on the strong influences of biology and critical periods of development in life that can have long-lasting influence on a person. Certain experiences early in life are considered crucial for life-long development, such as positive early attachment with a caregiver. This theory places value on observations in naturalistic settings.

- **Ecological Theory** focuses on environmental influences on human development. Urie Bronfenbrenner proposed five environmental systems that influence development. The theory explains a range of contexts that provide developmental influence as well as connections between these systems.

Kohlberg's Moral Developmental Theory

Lawrence Kohlberg presented six stages of universal moral development. Kohlberg continued that development moved across these stages as a person had opportunity to take the perspective of another person and reflect on the conflict between his or her current stage of moral reasoning and that of a person at a higher level of moral reasoning.

NOTE: Piaget's theory also included some focus on moral development.

Later Life Theories provide explanation of development that is particular to the later years and ending time of life. While the developmental factors described in these theories can occur at earlier stages of life, these factors are more associated with adults as they move into the later years of middle adulthood and then late adulthood.

- **Socioemotional Selectivity Theory**

  Laura Carstensen developed a theory that focus on the social and emotional development of older adults. She proposed that as people age, they place a high value on emotional satisfaction and devote more time to those relationships which are more rewarding for them. At the same time, they lessen interaction with individuals who have just peripheral social contact with them. This theory also emphasizes the two types of goals for older adults – knowledge-related and emotional.

- **Kubler Ross Stages of Dying** Elisabeth Kubler-Ross provided a model of the stages of death and dying. According to this model, a dying person as well as those close to him or her go through five developmental stages in dealing with the death. This model can also be applied to other life experiences of loss.

Table 1

This table provides an overview of the theories of lifespan development.

Category of Theory	Psychoanalytic	Cognitive	Behavioral	Biological-Contextual	Later Life
Focus	- Inner and unconscious drives and motives of a person as determining factors in a person's behavior and development. - Importance of early life experiences as important developmental foundations for later life.	- Development of thinking and cognitive understanding of the world that a person lives in. - Active construction of understanding.	- Human development as observable behavior that reflects what a person is learning. -Learning is through experience with the environment.	-Role of organic, genetic inheritance - Influences of environment and society-commonly considered to be the nurture side of influence in development.	-Explanation of development that is particular to the later years and ending time of life.
Theories & Description	-Freud: Role of Unconscious Sexual Drive -Erikson: Social Factors Life crises as turning point for development	-Piaget: Cognitive construction of world Striving to understand world -Vygotsky: Role of social interaction and cultural influence with cognitive development -Information Processing: Increasing capacity for processing of information	-Bandura: Behavior/person/cognition, and environment Learning through observation -Skinner: Consequences of behavior on probably future occurrence of behavior Operant conditioning	-Ethological: Strong influences of biology Critical periods of development Critical early life experiences -Ecological: Five environmental contexts that influence development -Kohlberg: Development of moral reasoning Consideration of perspective of others	-Socio-emotional Selectivity: ....Knowledge-related and emotional goals Movement in relationship focus from quantity to quality -Kubler-Ross: Five developmental stages in dealing with death or loss

Areas of Personal Development

Each person has multiple components of self in which he or she develops. These components are integrated into the whole person. All do not develop at the same rate through each lifespan stage. However course textbooks on lifespan development do provide norms for development to expect at each lifespan stage. When one of these components is not aligned well with the development in other components, there can be challenge to whole person functioning.

- **Cognitive Development** involves growth in a person's thought, intelligence and language. This development is evidenced by getting the most out of life by asking questions, being open to new ideas, learning new skills, and studying effectively.
- **Emotional Development** involves growth in understanding one's own emotions and the emotions of others. This development also involves growth in self-regulation of emotions and growth in facets of emotional well-being such as self-esteem, self-confidence, optimism, and satisfaction in relationships.
- **Moral Development** involves growth in a person's understanding and actions with rules and expectations on what should be done as people interact with each other.
- **Physical Development** involves growth and functioning of our bodies. This development is reflected through maintaining optimal health by getting enough sleep, eating healthy, exercising, and avoiding unhealthy habits. It can also be reflected through practice of negative health habits such as negligence of one's body or practice of habits that are harmful to one's physical health.
- **Social Development** involves growth and functioning of our relationships and interactions with other people. This development is evidenced in the quality and extent of supportive social networks, personal contributions to society, and treatment of cultural diversity.

Course textbooks discuss development of individuals in the above areas for each Lifespan stage. This workbook will facilitate student conceptualization of total person development in each of the following lifespan stages. The key focus of this workbook is exploration of theory application and the five areas of personal development for each of the following lifespan stages as covered in section IV..

Lifespan Stages

- Beginnings – Conception to Birth.
- Infancy – birth to 24 months.
- Early Childhood – 2 – 5 years.
- Middle to Late Childhood – 6 – 11 years.
- Adolescence – 12 – 20 years.
- Early Adulthood - 20s and 30s.
- Middle Adulthood – 40s and 50s.
- Late Adulthood – 60s and beyond
- Endings – Death

Reflections on Personal Development

Study of lifespan development can open the eyes and the insight of a student to his or her own development over the years. It is meaningful for students to reflect back and even compare self during childhood to their current lifespan stage per the discussion of those lifespan stages in their textbook. This section of the workbook provides exercises for students to do this self-reflection and also a template for a self case-study on lifespan development.

Conclusions on Application to Professional and Personal Life

While many degree programs require a course in lifespan development, this course can be extremely useful beyond just the credit hours for degree completion. This last section of the workbook provides resources and guidance for students to apply the workbook and course textbook contents to their own careers as well as work with other people in a personal modality such as with family or community work.

References

This list includes references integrated into the chapters of the workbook.

Chapter Organization – for each Chapter for a Theory, Area of Personal Development, or Lifespan Stage

As this is a workbook, many opportunities are also included to apply content learned through exercises, Practice Test Items, and use of additional resources such as website links or articles. Throughout the workbook, tips are provided for both instructors and students to enhance integration of this material into their course. The format for the chapters will be:

Background – This will provide background discussion on the respective theory or lifespan stage. The chapters on theories will focus on description of the theory, its founder, and the variables of influence it brings to lifespan development. The chapters on lifespan stages will provide a brief description of the stage and then discuss application of each theory to that lifespan stage.

Exercises– Each chapter includes exercises for students to apply concepts of the chapter in real-life situations.

Case Studies for Lifespan Stages –Each chapter on one of the lifespan stages will include a case study on an individual for that stage in which cognitive, emotional, moral, physical, and social factors are discussed and the person is discussed in light of the different theories.

Practice Test Items –Practice Test Items that include multiple choice, true/ false, and short answer items are usually available through .publishers of textbooks that are commonly used for courses in life-span development. The Practice Test Items that are included in this text are in essay format and require students to apply learned concepts to life situations, thus testing a student's capacity to translate knowledge into practice.

Additional Resources – Each chapter includes additional resources that can expand knowledge of content. These include links for websites, videos, articles, and classroom materials.

Tips for Instructors – Each chapter includes tips for instructor use of this chapter as integration in course work on lifespan development.

Tips for Students– Each chapter includes tips for student use of chapter information for integration into course study or life application.

Exercises

The exercises on the following pages provide opportunity for the student to apply theoretical concepts to life as they experience it and as they observe the experienced life of others.

Exercise One – Theories - Worksheet on Developmental Theories

This Worksheet provides an overview of developmental theories as applied to each life-span stage. As you describe application to a life-span stage, the key is to identify examples of how a person in that life-span stage would exhibit that theory. The answers will probably not be in black and white in your course textbook. Instead, you will need to take the general concept of the theory and identify how that looks in each life-span stage.

1. **Freud-**
   a. Describe Freud's Developmental Theory
   b. Describe application to Infancy and Early Childhood.
   c. Describe application to Middle and Late Childhood.
   d. Describe application to Adolescence.
   e. Describe application to Early Adulthood.
   f. Describe application to Middle Adulthood.
   g. Describe application to Late Adulthood.

2. **Erikson-**
   a. Describe Erikson's Developmental Theory.
   b. Describe application to Infancy and Early Childhood.
   c. Describe application to Middle and Late Childhood.
   d. Describe application to Adolescence.
   e. Describe application to Early Adulthood.
   f. Describe application to Middle Adulthood.
   g. Describe application to Late Adulthood.

3. **Piaget-**
   a. Describe Piaget's Developmental Theory.
   b. Describe application to Infancy and Early Childhood.

c. Describe application to Middle and Late Childhood.
d. Describe application to Adolescence.
e. Describe application to Early Adulthood.
f. Describe application to Middle Adulthood.
g. Describe application to Late Adulthood.

4.Vygotsky-

a. Describe Vygotsky's Developmental Theory.
b. Describe application to Infancy and Early Childhood.
c. Describe application to Middle and Late Childhood.
d. Describe application to Adolescence
e. Describe application to Early Adulthood.
f. Describe application to Middle Adulthood.
g. Describe application to Late Adulthood.

5. Information-Processing Theory-

a. Describe the Information –Processing Developmental Theory.
b. Describe application to Infancy and Early Childhood.
c. Describe application to Middle and Late Childhood.
d. Describe application to Adolescence
e. Describe application to Early Adulthood.
f. Describe application to Middle Adulthood.
g. Describe application to Late Adulthood.

6. Bandura –

a. Describe Bandura's Social Cognitive Theory.
b. Describe application to Infancy and Early Childhood.
c. Describe application to Middle and Late Childhood.
d. Describe application to Adolescence.
e. Describe application to Early Adulthood.
f. Describe application to Middle Adulthood.
g. Describe application to Late Adulthood.

7. Skinner -

a. Describe Operant Conditioning Theory.
b. Describe application to Infancy and Early Childhood.
c. Describe application to Middle and Late Childhood.
d. Describe application to Adolescence.
e. Describe application to Early Adulthood.
f. Describe application to Middle Adulthood.
g. Describe application to Late Adulthood.

8. Ethological -

a. Describe the Ethological Theory.
b. Describe application to Infancy and Early Childhood.
c. Describe application to Middle and Late Childhood.
d. Describe application to Adolescence.
e. Describe application to Early Adulthood.
f. Describe application to Middle Adulthood.
g. Describe application to Late Adulthood.

9. Ecological -

a. Describe the Ecological Theory.
b. Describe application to Infancy and Early Childhood.
c. Describe application to Middle and Late Childhood.
d. Describe application to Adolescence.
e. Describe application to Early Adulthood.
f. Describe application to Middle Adulthood.
g. Describe application to Late Adulthood.

10. Kohlberg –

a. Describe Kohlberg's Moral Reasoning Theory.
b. Describe application to Infancy and Early Childhood.
c. Describe application to Middle and Late Childhood.
d. Describe application to Adolescence.
e. Describe application to Early Adulthood.

f. Describe application to Middle Adulthood.
g. Describe application to Late Adulthood.

11. Socioemotional Selectivity Theory:

a. Describe the Socioemotional Selectivity theory.
b. Describe application of the theory to Middle Adulthood
c. Describe application of the theory to Late Adulthood

12. Kubler-Ross' Stages of Dying:

List and describe the five stages of dying in the Kubler-Ross Model. Be able to describe how you would know that a person is each of the stages.

Where Do You Stand on Major Developmental Issues?

Explorations Exercise page 31

Sigelman, C.K. & Rider, E.A. (2009) *Life-span human development.* (6th ed.) Belmont, CA: Wadsworth Cengage Learning

Compare Yourself with the Theories

Table 2.4, page 54

Sigelman, C.K. & Rider, E.A. (2009) *Life-span human development.* Belmont, CA: Wadsworth Cengage Learning

Case Study

Using Developmental Theories to Prevent Teenage Pregnancy

Explorations Exercise page 53

Sigelman, C.K. & Rider, E.A. (2009) *Life-span human development.* Belmont, CA: Wadsworth Cengage Learning

Practice Test Items

1. Freud

As Freud developed his theory, much of his insight was gained through work with his patients, many of whom had experienced childhood abuse and had also repressed the traumatic experiences of this. Sally is a 45 year old female who was sexually abused by her grandfather when she was five to seven years of age. Through your knowledge of Freud's theory, describe some potential consequences for Sally that could represent each of these.

a. A Defense Mechanism
b. Regression

2. Erikson

Reflect on your own life to your current life stage. List the Erikson stages that you have gone through and discuss comparison of yourself to that stage.

3. Piaget

Last year, when her aunt visited, baby, Jawana simply grasped toys and sucked on them, sometimes hitting them against the table repeatedly. This year she has many more capabilities, such as drawing and using some words. What has changed cognitively since last she when she was in Piaget's earlier substage of development. How would Piaget explain how those changes occurred?

4. Vygotsky

Vygotsky considered social and cultural activities to be an integral part of development.

Describe the essence of his theory and then discuss how you have used the inventions of society in your own cognitive development.

5. Information-Processing

The Information-Processing theory has been likened to a computer. Think about <u>one</u> of the following rote actions that you now take on probably a daily basis and describe application of these steps of the Information-Processing theory to your learning of that rote action: Input; Encoding; Memory; Retrieval, and Executive Controls.

a. Driving your vehicle
b. Brushing your teeth
c. Taking a bath
d. Eating soup

6. Bandura

Bandura's early research had priority of focus on learning through observation. Briefly describe this part of his Social Cognitive Theory and then discuss how this has been a part of your own cognitive development.

7. Skinner

As a mathematics teacher, you have concerns about your students' ability with time on task. Almost daily, you assign them problems from their textbook to work on for a period of thirty minutes. You notice that very few students in the class actually work on the problems for those thirty minutes. Many students will try to do something else after only a portion of that time, such as doodle or try to talk to a classmate. Describe methods that you could use for each of the following consequences with Skinner's theory to increase students' time on task to the desired thirty minutes.

a. Positive Reinforcement
b. Negative Reinforcement
c. Presentation Punishment
d. Removal Punishment

8. Ethological

Attachment and imprinting are two concepts in Ethological theory that focus on the experience of the first year of life and consequences from that on the rest of life. Describe these two concepts and how these have been represented in your own life to this point.

Choose one of the following aspects of Ethological theory and describe how that was represented in your own life.

a. Attachment to your caregiver in your first year of life and consequences in your life to this point in your life.
b. Imprinting as rapid, innate learning that involves attachment to the first moving object.

9. Ecological

Look back at your own development in childhood during your years of elementary through high school. Define and Describe each of the following systems that were present for you during those years. Your description should be what was unique to you, not just a repeat of the definition of that system.

a. Microsystem
b. Mesosystem
c. Exosystem
d. Macrosystem
e. Chronosystem

10. Kohlberg

Describe Kohlberg's three levels and six stages of moral development.

a. Discuss which of the stages you believe yourself to be in and why.
b. Choose a famous person such as a political leader, professional athlete, or entertainer and discuss which of the stages you believe that person to be in and why.

11. Socioemotional Selectivity Theory

The Socioemotional Selectivity Theory focuses on the tendency for older adults to become more selective about their social networks. Describe the essence of this theory. Then choose an older adult that you know and discuss how you have seen this theory apply in that person's life.

12. Kubler-Ross' Stages of Dying

List in order the five stages of grieving in the Kubler-Ross model. Think of someone who has experienced a loss (death or other loss) in life. Discuss how the person may have gone through these stages with that loss.

Additional Resources

Textbooks

Santrock, J. (2015). *Life-span development*. (15th ed.). Boston: McGraw-Hill Publishers. NOTE: McGraw-Hill also offers an online resource to accompany this text- *Connect.*

Sigelman, C.K. & Rider, E.A. (2014). *Life-span human development* (8th ed.). Belmont, CA: Wadsworth Cengage Learning.

Web Links

https://www.verywell.com/major-developmental-theorists-2795093

http://www.slideshare.net/peningry/theories-of-human-development

http://study.com/academy/lesson/behavioral-cognitive-developmental-social-cognitive-constructivist-perspectives.html

https://www.youtube.com/watch?v=qidnwbOhTus&feature=youtu.be

https://www.youtube.com/watch?v=WMv8A9qg6jY

Tips for Instructors

While students may easily learn rote facts about the theories, they can better learn application of the theories to life-span development through opportunities for application. Examples are provided in this chapter and with each chapter on the theories for exam items and assignments that can promote integration of theory to life.

Tips for Students

These theories of life-span development provide core understanding of why we live the way we live. To borrow a concept from health care, understanding involves identification of the evidence. As you apply a theory to your life or the life of someone else, think about what is the evidence that you or the other person is representing that facet of that theory.

CHAPTER 2

Theories

Psychoanalytic Theories

Background

Psychoanalytic theories are among the older theories of human development. These focus on the inner and unconscious drives and motives of a person as determining factors in a person's behavior and development. Behavior is seen as being symbolic of the inner workings of a person's mind. These theories also emphasize the importance of early life experiences, especially with parents as important developmental foundations for later life. The Psychoanalytic theories covered here provide stages of development that have alignment with chronological ages and stages of development.

Exercises

1. Compare and Contrast Essay/Paper

In one paragraph for each theory, describe the core construct of Freud's theory and of Erikson's theory. Then provide a paragraph describing each of the following:

a. Strengths
   i. Freud
   ii. Erikson

b. Weaknesses
   i. Freud
   ii. Erikson

c. How Freud's theory and Erikson's theory are alike

d. How Freud's theory and Erikson's theory are different

2. **Application for Today**

Choose one of the following current issues of society and explain the difference in a Freud view and a Erikson view of the issue.

a. Bullying of HS girl in bathroom
b. Pornography
c. School shooting
d. Politics
e. Religious

Practice Test Items

1. As babies are born, there seems to be an ever-present debate on the merits of a new mom breast-feeding her baby or not. Choose one side of this issue and present rationale for your stance by explanation from both Freud's theory and Erikson's theory.

2. You are a parent of a 15 month old and know it is time to address the issue of toilet training. What are considerations from both Freud and Erikson that would guide your decision in how to manage this for your 15 month old.

3. Sometimes a male child or adult is referred to as a "Mama's boy" and sometimes a female child or adult is referred to as a "Daddy's girl." Describe how Freud's theory would fit this. Also describe how Erikson's stages 3 – 5 would fit this.

4. Think of yourself in elementary school, first through 4th grade. Describe how both Freud's and Erikson's theory fit you during those years.

Additional Resources

Textbooks

Santrock, J. (2015). *Life-span development.* (15th ed.). Boston: McGraw-Hill Publishers. NOTE: McGraw-Hill also offers an online resource to accompany this text- *Connect.*

Sigelman, C.K. & Rider, E.A. (2014). *Life-span human development* (8th ed.). Belmont, CA: Wadsworth Cengage Learning.

Web Links

https://www.youtube.com/watch?v=gE55soly70M

https://www.youtube.com/watch?v=i3OeY2EZDi0

https://www.youtube.com/watch?v=paJDIC7k6s4

http://www.earlychildhoodnews.com/earlychildhood/article_view.aspx?ArticleID=411

This early childhood news site has an interesting article on applying understanding of developmental theories to teaching. It highlights how understanding these theories may impact our work in education. The article offers scenarios of how a teacher would respond to a situation differently when considering a different theory.

http://www.gulfbend.org/poc/view_doc.php?type=doc&id=7924..

This source provided additional information about some of the theories covered in this book and your course texts.

Tips for Instructors

While students may easily learn rote facts about the theories, they can better learn application of the theories to life-span development through opportunities for application. Examples are provided in this chapter and with each chapter on the theories for exam items and assignments that can promote integration of theory to life.

Tips for Students

These theories of life-span development provide core understanding of why we live the way we live. To borrow a concept from health care, understanding involves identification of the evidence. As you apply a theory to your life or the life of someone else, think about what is the evidence that you or the other person is representing that facet of that theory.

Theory of Freud

Background on Sigmund Freud

Sigmund Freud's theory provide a foundation for most of the counseling and psychological theories practiced today. He focused on the role of the unconscious in human development. Much of his work explored conflicts that a person experience between their inner drives and life expectations from the world around them. Freud believed that sexual drive was the primary motivation for human behavior. Freud's stages are known as psychosexual stages as Freud believed that the focus of pleasure and sexual impulses shifted over life to different parts of the body – this is reflected in the name of stages in this theory. Later psychoanalytic theorists provided explanation of human development that moved away from Freud's emphasis on sexual instincts. Freud's theory includes stages from birth through puberty. The last stage begins with puberty and lasts for the rest of life.

Table 2 Freud's Stages of Development

Stage	Age	Description of Stage
Oral	First year Of life	Focus is on need for food and pleasure – basic nurturing. Major activity of infant ins nursing from mom or a bottle. Major source of pleasure is centered on the mouth.
Anal	1 – 3 years old	Functioning of the anal physical zone becomes a focus, such as learning to manage one's own urination and defecation, thus learning independence, sense of personal power, and capacity to express negative feelings one has. Major source of pleasure centers on the anus.
Phallic	3 – 6 years old	Focus on love for opposite sex parent. Sense of sexuality begins to emerge during this stage. Major source of pleasure centers on the genitals.
Latency	6 – 12 years old	Interest moves from focus on sexuality to interest in school, sports, friends, play, and overall socialization with others. Major source of pleasure centers on social and intellectual skills.
Genital	12 years Through Adulthood	Sexual energy emerges with puberty and is present until and through senility. Sexual energy can be invested in socially acceptable activities such as sports or the arts. Adults move toward freedom from parents and engagement in love and work. Major source of pleasure come from someone outside the family.
Theme across stages: Adult personality is developed through way a person manages conflict between source of pleasure and real life demands at each of the above stages.		

Exercises

1. Journaling – Begin a journal as you studies the theories of lifespan development and write reflections about yourself for each theory and stage studies. For Freud's theory, describe what you remember about yourself for each of the stages of this theory. Then reflect on how your memories correlate with the description of that stage of Freud's theory.

2. Observation - Use your journal to take notes from observation of people who are currently in each of the stages of Freud's theory. As with yourself, note how the person demonstrates the applicable stage or not. For example, common terms used for the Phallic stage may be a girl who is a "Daddy's girl" or a boy who is a "Mamma's boy." If you know a child who is between 3 and 5 years of age and fits that, how does that status fit Freud's description of the Phallic stage?

3. Research – Find a scholarly article on Freud's stages of life and summarize that to share with your class. Focus on what the article teaches you about Freud's theory and how you can apply that to your life and work.

4. Developmental Problems – As with most theories, Freud proposed the usual way a person will develop. As noted in the table above, conflicts can occur between the stage source of pleasure and what the person encounters in real life. Identify examples of such a conflict that should occur at each of the five stages of Freud's theory. For example, do you know a young girl who has been "Daddy's girl" and her parents divorce and she now lives with the mother while her dad is living with his new girl-friend? What issues do you see with that girl's life right now?

5. Application to Life and Work – Reflect on application of Freud's theory to your own life and work right now.
   a. How does the description of the stage you are in fit your own life now?
   b. How does this theory fit with the work that you do or that you plan to do?
   c. How does this theory fit with the significant other people in your life – family, best friends, co-workers, life partners, etc?

Case Study

Terry is a six year old boy and his sister Rachel is nine years old. Their mother is 29 years old and teaches third grade in the local elementary school. Their dad is 33 years old and a maintenance supervisor for the city housing authority. He has responsibility for six different housing complexes. The family has always seemed to be close to each other with parents and children spending a lot of time together at home as well as recreation together such as sports events. Recently the mother found out that the father had been having an affair with the next door neighbor. Ultimately, the parents get a divorce, with both children continuing to live with the mother. At this time, dad has visitation rights, but is not choosing to have any contact with the children. Terry seems to be adjusting without notable issues, but Rachel has several obvious issues. She has been academically successful at school, but now is getting failing grades on assignments, mom complains that she is constantly rebellious at home, and mom has recently enrolled Rachel in counseling services.

Reflection Questions:

1. How does this case seem to fit with Freud's theory for Terry, Rachel, the mother, and the father?

2. Both children in this case are in the age range for the Latency stage. Reflect on what issues might be different if Terry and/or Rachel were in one of the following stages.
   a. Oral
   b. Anal
   c. Phallic
   d. Genital

Practice Test Items

1. Describe the behavioral demonstration that you could observe in a person in each of the five stages of Freud's theory.

2. Describe the communication that you could observe in a person in each of the five stages of Freud's theory.

3. Describe some thoughts or thinking patterns that you could observe in a person in each of the five stages of Freud's theory.

4. Describe what a parent or caregiver could do to help a child develop successfully through each of the five stages of Freud's theory.

Additional Resources

Textbooks

Santrock, J. (2015). *Life-span development.* (15th ed.). Boston: McGraw-Hill Publishers. NOTE: McGraw-Hill also offers an online resource to accompany this text- *Connect.*

Sigelman, C.K. & Rider, E.A. (2014). *Life-span human development* (8th ed.). Belmont, CA: Wadsworth Cengage Learning.

Web Links

http://www.muskingum.edu/~psych/psycweb/history/freud.htm.

This video shows exactly how Freud came about with the different stages of development. It describes each stage and exactly what is meant by each and every stage.

https://youtu.be/cvOoYX45G_0

This can help you learn even more about Freud's theory and help discover more about what he means by his stages of development in children.

Tips for Instructors

While students may easily learn rote facts about the theories, they can better learn application of the theories to life-span development through opportunities for application. Examples are provided in this chapter and with each chapter on the theories for exam items and assignments that can promote integration of theory to life.

Tips for Students

These theories of life-span development provide core understanding of why we live the way we live. To borrow a concept from health care, understanding involves identification of the evidence. As you apply a theory to your life or the life of someone else, think about what is the evidence that you or the other person is representing that facet of that theory.

Theory of Erik Erikson

Background on Erik Erikson

Erik Erikson built on Freud's theory through a focus on social factors as primary motivation for development. His theory presented certain psychological and social tasks that a person should master at each lifespan stage of development. This theory frames these tasks as crises that are presented – Santrock (2015) explains these also as turning points in life. According to this theory, a person makes a life choice and resolves the crisis to move forward to the next stage with healthy development or does not resolve the crisis and moves forward with some developmental challenges. Erikson's theory provides stages from Infancy through Late Adulthood and are known as Psychosocial stages.

Table 3 Erikson's Stages of Development

Life-Span Stage and Age Range	Name of Stage	Crisis Turning Point Of the Stage
Infancy First year of life	**Trust vs Mistrust**	Development of trust as foundation that world will be okay to live in.
Infancy 1 to 3 years	**Autonomy vs Shame and Doubt**	Development of sense of independence and one's personal will. Shame and doubt could develop from excessive restraint or punishment.
Early Child-hood 3 to 5 years	**Initiative vs Guilt**	Development of active, purposeful, and responsible behavior. Guilt could develop from irresponsibility of child or excessive feelings of anxiety.
Middle and Late Child-hood 6 years to puberty	**Industry vs Inferiority**	Direction of energy toward mastery of knowledge and intellectual skills. Sense of inferiority could develop if child felt incompetent or unproductive.
Adolescence 10 to 20 years	**Identity vs Identity Confu-sion**	Exploration of who one is and discernment of a life pathway to follow. Identity con-fusion occurs when one does not develop a positive identity.

Early Adulthood 20s and 30s	**Intimacy vs Isolation**	Development of healthy friendships and an intimate relationship with another person. Failure to develop these can result in isolation.
Middle Adulthood 40s and 50s	**Generativity vs Stagnation**	Focus on helping younger generations to develop and lead useful lives. Stagnation occurs when one feels like he or she has not done anything to help younger generations.
Late Adulthood 60s onward	**Integrity vs Despair**	Focus on reflection of the past life lived. Integrity represents a sense of a life well lived. A sense of despair results when one feels life has been wasted to some extent.

Exercises

1. Journaling – Begin a journal as you study the theories of lifespan development and write reflections about yourself for each theory and stage studies. For Erikson's theory, describe what you remember about yourself for each of the stages of this theory up to the stage that you are now in. Then reflect on how your memories correlate with the description of that stage of Erikson's theory. Also think ahead to the stages of Erikson's theory that are yet to be experienced. Think about the potential alternatives that could fit that stage of your life. How can you prepare and manage your life to have the positive alternative at that time.

2. Observation - Use your journal to take notes from observation of people who are currently in each of the stages of Erikson's theory. As with yourself, note how the person demonstrates the applicable stage or not. For example, how might a child of nine demonstrate a sense of industry or a sense of inferiority in the setting of school?

3. Research – Find a scholarly article on Erikson's stages of life and summarize that to share with your class. Focus on what the article teaches you about Erikson's theory and how you can apply that to your life and work.

4. Developmental Problems – As with most theories, Erikson proposed the usual way a person will develop. As noted in the table above, a a unique task of development will occur that requires some crisis resolution. Identify examples of such a task and crisis that could occur

at each of the five stages of Erikson's theory.

5. Application to Life and Work – Reflect on application of Erikson's theory to your own life and work right now.

    a. How does the description of the stage you are in fit your own life now?
    b. How does this theory fit with the work that you do or that you plan to do?
    c. How does this theory fit with the significant other people in your life – family, best friends, co-workers, life partners, etc?

Case Study

Terry is a six year old boy and his sister Rachel is nine years old. Their mother is 29 years old and teaches third grade in the local elementary school. Their dad is 33 years old and a maintenance supervisor for the city housing authority. He has responsibility for six different housing complexes. The family has always seemed to be close to each other with parents and children spending a lot of time together at home as well as recreation together such as sports events. Recently the mother found out that the father had been having an affair with the next door neighbor. Ultimately, the parents get a divorce, with both children continuing to live with the mother. At this time, dad has visitation rights, but is not choosing to have any contact with the children. Terry seems to be adjusting without notable issues, but Rachel has several obvious issues. She has been academically successful at school, but now is getting failing grades on assignments, mom complains that she is constantly rebellious at home, and mom has recently enrolled Rachel in counseling services.

Reflection Questions:

1. How does this case seem to fit with Erikson's theory for Terry, Rachel, the mother, and the father?

2. Both children in this case are in the age range for the Industry versus Inferiority stage. Reflect on what issues might be present for them in this stage and also what could be present for Rachel as she enters the next stage of Identity versus Identity Confusion next year as she has her 10th birthday.

Practice Test Items

1. Describe the behavioral demonstration that you could observe in a person in each of the eight stages of Erikson's theory.

2. Describe the communication that you could observe in a person in each of the eight stages of Erikson's theory.

3. Describe some thoughts or thinking patterns that you could observe in a person in each of the eight stages of Erikson's theory.

4. Describe what a parent or caregiver could do to help a child develop successfully through each of the eight stages of Erikson's theory.

Additional Resources

Textbooks

Santrock, J. (2015). *Life-span development.* (15th ed.). Boston: McGraw-Hill Publishers. NOTE: McGraw-Hill also offers an online resource to accompany this text- *Connect.*

Sigelman, C.K. & Rider, E.A. (2014). *Life-span human development* (8th ed.). Belmont, CA: Wadsworth Cengage Learning.

Web Links

http://www.esplorepsychoogy.com/eriksons-eight-stages-of-psychosocial-development/

This resource gave additional information into Erikson's eight stages of Psychosocial Development. It listed the eight steps in a chart and then described the stages in detail. This allowed me to better choose what stage was child was in.

www.simplypsychology.org/Erik-Erikson.html

This resource provides basic information on Erikson's theory. Information is available at www.simplepsychology.org on other theories of life-span development as well. .

https://youtu.be/Iz-AeGMhzV0

This YouTube video b is a fun resource using popular childrens' movies to describe Erikson's 8 stages of development showing the stages in action.

https://www.youtube.com/watch?v=grSxCdtLl38

This video explains each stage of Erikson's theory in detailed and explains various myths people speak upon in life. The video provides a brief description and explains that some of the behavior is not proven, but is a myth.

Tips for Instructors

While students may easily learn rote facts about the theories, they can better learn application of the theories to life-span development through opportunities for application. Examples are provided in this chapter and with each chapter on the theories for exam items and assignments that can promote integration of theory to life.

Tips for Students

These theories of life-span development provide core understanding of why we live the way we live. To borrow a concept from health care, understanding involves identification of the evidence. As you apply a theory to your life or the life of someone else, think about what is the evidence that you or the other person is representing that facet of that theory.

Cognitive Theories

Background

Cognitive theories emphasize the development of thinking and cognitive understanding of the world that a person lives in. Santrock (2015) noted that the cognitive theories emphasize a person's active construction of understanding. Sigelman and Rider (2014) that throughout life, we are engaged in acquisition of knowledge and in problem solving. However, their minds can change in important ways. Mind can be thought of as the process in which the physical brain engages as we perceive, think, choose, remember, etc. As a person makes sense of his world, he takes this understanding in the mind and then interacts with his world. The three theories that will be covered in this section are Piaget's Constructivist Approach, Vygotsky's Sociocultural Model, and the Information Processing Approach.

Table 4 Cognitive Theories of Development

Founder	Theory	Description of Theory
Jean Piaget	Cognitive Development Theory	Cognitive development includes 4 stages in which individuals actively construct their understanding of the world. Intelligence is considered to be a basic function of life to facilitate the adaptation of an organism to its environment.
Lev Vygotsky	SocioculturalCognitive Theory	Knowledge is actively constructed through the guidance of social interaction and culture. Individuals learn to use the inventions of society and interact with more-skilled adults as they develop cognitively. These influences could promote differences in cognitive development between societies.
Robert Siegler	Information-Processing Theory	Individuals gradually develop increased capacity for processing information. This then supports acquisition of increasingly complex knowledge and skills. Individuals manipulate, monitor, and strategize information with central processes of thinking and memory. This theory is likened to the operation of a computer.

Exercises

1. Compare and Contrast Essay/Paper

In one paragraph for each theory, describe the core construct of the theories of Piaget, Vygotsky, and Information-Processing theory. Then provide a paragraph describing each of the following:

a. Strengths
   i. Piaget
   ii. Vygotsky
   ii. Information-Processing

b. Weaknesses
   i. Piaget
   ii. Vygotsky
   iii. Information-Processing

c. How the theories of Piaget, Vygotsky, and Information Processing are alike

d. How the theories of Piaget, Vygotsky, and Information Processing are different

2. Application for Today

Choose one of the following areas of knowledge/skill and explain how each of the theories of Piaget, Vygotsky, and Information Processing would describe that development.

a. An eye on top of an electric stove is hot and will burn if one touches it when it is red.
b. A woman tries on a dress to see if it meets her employer's dress code of being long enough to cover her knees.
c. Playing basketball
d. Mathematical operations in Geometry
e. Conduct of marriage ceremonies

Practice Test Items

1. Complete each of the following sentences by entering the name of one of the three theories (Piaget, Vygotsky, or Information-Processing) in the blank. After completing the sentence, provide a short explanation of why that answer would be the best fit.

    a. For generations, the women in the Smith family have cut the ends of a ham off before baking it. This learned behavior would be an example of the ____________________theory.

    b. Four-year old Jessie enjoys family trips to McDonald's restaurant. As mom is helping him learn the alphabet, each time they come to the capital letter "M," Jessie claps his hands and says "Yea – McDonald's and a hamburger." This is representative of ___________ theory. Which stage in that theory would this fit?

    c. Susan steps outside her house to go to her car and drive to work. She stops for a minute, looks around and then returns into the house to get an umbrella. This is representative of the ____________________ theory.

2. Explain how each of the following theories frame the construction of understanding.
    a. Piaget
    b. Vygotsky
    c. Information Processing

3. Using integration of all three theories (Piaget, Vygotsky, or Information-Processing), describe how a 21 year old male would decide what vehicle to purchase as the first vehicle he ever owned.

4. Describe how you used all three theories (Piaget, Vygotsky, or Information-Processing) to complete high school.

Additional Resources

Textbooks

Santrock, J. (2015). *Life-span development.* (15th ed.). Boston: McGraw-Hill Publishers. NOTE: McGraw-Hill also offers an online resource to accompany this text- *Connect.*

Sigelman, C.K. & Rider, E.A. 2014). *Life-span human development* (8th ed.). Belmont, CA: Wadsworth Cengage Learning.

Web Links

http://highered.mheducation.com/sites/0072820144/student_view0/chapter1/index.html

http://www.simplypsychology.org/developmental-psychology.html

http://psychology.about.com/od/developmentstudyguide/p/devthinkers.htm

http://study.com/academy/lesson/differences-between-piaget-vygotskys-cognitive-

development-theories.html

http://www.oakton.edu/user/1/dmalone/PiagetVygot.pdf

Tips for Instructors

While students may easily learn rote facts about the theories, they can better learn application of the theories to life-span development through opportunities for application. Examples are provided in this chapter and with each chapter on the theories for exam items and assignments that can promote integration of theory to life.

Tips for Students

These theories of life-span development provide core understanding of why we live the way we live. To borrow a concept from health care, understanding involves identification of the evidence. As you apply a theory to your life or the life of someone else, think about what is the evidence that you or the other person is representing that facet of that theory.

Jean Piaget's Cognitive Developmental Theory

Background

Jean Piaget presented four stages of development through which children cognitively construct their world. Piaget proposed that cognitive development changes over these stages as a child constantly strives to understand his world (Woolfolk and Perry, 2015). This is done as a person gathers information and then organizes that information. Piaget's four stages of development begin with birth and conclude with a developmental stage beginning at age 11 and continuation through adulthood. Piaget's theory also included aspects of moral development.

Table 5 Piaget's Stages of Cognitive Development

Stage	Age	Description
Sensorimotor	Birth to 2 years	An infant coordinates sensory experiences with physical actions to construct an understanding of the world he or she lives in. There is demonstration of the reflexes of instinct after birth to a beginning of symbolic thought by two years.
Preoperational	2 to 7 years	A child will begin to use words and images to demonstrate increased symbolic thinking to represent the world.
Concrete Operational	7 to 11 years	The child shows development of logical reasoning about concrete events and can now perform operations that involve objects.
Formal Operational	11 years throughout adulthood	Development grows to include reasoning that is abstract, idealistic, and logical. This is demonstrated through thoughts about the future, problem solving, and systematic development and testing of hypotheses.

Exercises

1. Journaling – Begin a journal as you studies the theories of lifespan development and write reflections about yourself for each theory and stage studies. For Piaget's theory, describe what you remember about yourself for each of the stages of this theory. Then reflect on how your memories correlate with the description of that stage of Piaget's theory.

2. Observation - Use your journal to take notes from observation of people who are currently in each of the stages of Piaget's theory. As with yourself, note how the person demonstrates the applicable stage or not. For example, how might a child playing with dolls or toy soldiers relate to one of Piaget's theories?

3. Research – Find a scholarly article on Piaget's stages of life and summarize that to share with your class. Focus on what the article teaches you about Piaget's theory and how you can apply that to your life and work.

4. Developmental Problems – As with most theories, Piaget proposed the usual way a person will develop cognitively. Find some information to share with your class on application of Piaget's theory with Learning Disabilities or Mental Retardation.

5. Application to Life and Work – Reflect on application of Piaget's theory to your own life and work right now.

   f. How does the description of the stage you are in fit your own life now?

   g. How does this theory fit with the work that you do or that you plan to do?

   h. How does this theory fit with the significant other people in your life – family, best friends, co-workers, life partners, etc?

Case Study

Jaelyn is two years old. Last year, when her aunt visited, baby Jaelyn simply grasped toys and sucked on them, sometimes hitting them against the table repeatedly. This year she has many more capabilities, such as drawing and using some words.

Reflection Questions

1. What Piaget stage was she in last year?

2. What has changed cognitively since last she when she was in Piaget's earlier stage of development.

3. What Piaget stage of development is Jaelyn in this year?

4. How would Piaget explain how those changes occurred?

Practice Test Items

1. Describe the behavioral demonstration that you could observe in a person in each of the five stages of Piaget's theory.

2. Describe the communication that you could observe in a person in each of the five stages of Piaget's theory.

3. Describe some thoughts or thinking patterns that you could observe in a person in each of the five stages of Piaget's theory.

4. Describe what a parent or caregiver could do to help a child develop successfully through each of the five stages of Piaget's theory.

Additional Resources

Textbooks

Santrock, J. (2013). *Life-span development.* (15th ed.). Boston: McGraw-Hill Publishers. NOTE: McGraw-Hill also offers an online resource to accompany this text- *Connect.*

Sigelman, C.K. & Rider, E.A. (2014). *Life-span human development* (8th ed.). Belmont, CA: Wadsworth Cengage Learning.

Web Links

http://www.webmd.com/children/piaget-stages-of-development

http://youtube/0dXV6ol-z3w

https://www.youtube.com/watch?v=TRF27F2bn-A

https://www.youtube.com/watch?v=0XwjIruMI94

https://www.google.com/?gws_rd=ssl#q=PPT+on+Piaget

Tips for Instructors

While students may easily learn rote facts about the theories, they can better learn application of the theories to life-span development through opportunities for application. Examples are provided in this chapter and with each chapter on the theories for exam items and assignments that can promote integration of theory to life.

Tips for Students

These theories of life-span development provide core understanding of why we live the way we live. To borrow a concept from health care, understanding involves identification of the evidence. As you apply a theory to your life or the life of someone else, think about what is the evidence that you or the other person is representing that facet of that theory.

Vygotsky's Sociocultural Cognitive Theory

Background

Leo Vygotsky also believed that children actively construct knowledge about their world. He emphasized the roles of social interaction and cultural influence in cognitive development. Vygotsky's theory provided a framework of learning through interaction and influence of their social and cultural worlds. Two key concepts of Vygotsky's theory are the Zone of Proximal Development and Tools of One's Culture. The Zone of Proximal Development is that gap between what a person can learn independently and what the person can learn with guidance and encouragement from a person more skilled than himself. This guidance is given in a process called Scaffolding in which the initial guidance may be very direct and specific. As the learner increases competence, less specific guidance is given. The tools of culture include language of a culture, memory strategies, strategies for learning, and inventions such as educational games or devises to assist learning. Vygotsky's theory is not organized into specific stages per certain chronological age, but rather provides a framework that could apply to any lifespan stage.

Figure 1 Vygotsky's Theory of Social Interaction and Culture Influence on Cognitive Development.

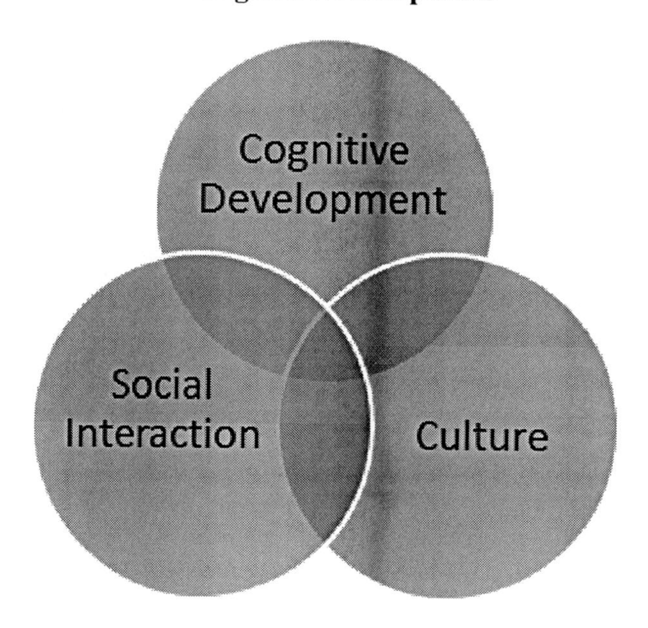

Exercises

1. Journaling – Begin a journal as you studies the theories of lifespan development and write reflections about yourself for each theory and stage studied. For Vygotsky's theory, describe what you remember about yourself on the influences of social interaction and culture in your development through life to where you are now.

2. Observation - Use your journal to take notes from observation of people who are at each of the different life-span stages and from different environmental backgrounds from your own. As with yourself, note how the person demonstrates influence of their culture and social interactions in development.

3. Research – Find a scholarly article on Vygotsky's theory of development and summarize that to share with your class. Focus on what the article teaches you about Vygotsky's theory and how you can apply that to your life and work.

4. Developmental Problems – Sometimes a person has a life change that moves him or her into a different cultural setting or into different social interactions. Reflect on each of the following and describe developmental challenges that could occur in view of Vygotsky's theory.

   a. A couple from the United States adopts a 3 year old girl from a Russian orphanage. Discuss challenges for both the couple and the adopted daughter.

   b. A high school senior female is head cheerleader and was this year's homecoming queen. In November, her dad accepts a call to pastor a church in the different part of the state and the family moves with her now finishing her senior year and high school in a different location.

   c. Terrence Duvall is a 44 year old black male who just retired from the U.S. Marine Corps and has moved back to his hometown and is looking for a job with which he hopes to work long enough to earn a second retirement.

5. Application to Life and Work – Reflect on application of Vygotsky's theory to your own life and work right now.

   a. How does the description of the stage you are in fit your own life now?

b. How does this theory fit with the work that you do or that you plan to do?

c. How does this theory fit with the significant other people in your life – family, best friends, co-workers, life partners, etc?

Case Study

Sigelman and Rider (2014) share this case that has application to Vygotsky's theory.

Annie, a 4-year old, receives her first jigsaw puzzle for her birthday. She attempts to work on the puzzle, but gets nowhere, until her father sits down beside her and gives her some tips. He suggests that it would be a good idea to put the corners together first. He points to the pink area at the edge of one corner piece and says " Let's look for another pink piece." When Annie seems frustrated, he places two interlocking pieces near each other so that she will notice them. And when she succeeds, he offers words of encouragement. As Annie gets the hang if it, he..............." (p. 210).

Reflection Questions

1. Describe the Zone of Proximal Development that exists in this case.

2. What are the levels of Scaffolding that you see in this case?

3. How would you complete the last sentence for this scenario to continue demonstration of Scaffolding to facilitate the Zone of Proximal Development for Annie?

Practice Test Items

1. Describe the behavioral demonstration that you could observe in a person in Vygotsky's theory.

2. Describe the communication that you could observe in a person in Vygotsky's theory.

3. Describe some thoughts or thinking patterns that you could observe in a person in Vygotsky's theory.

4. Describe what a parent or caregiver could do to help a child develop successfully through Vygotsky's theory.

Additional Resources

Textbooks

Santrock, J. (2013). *Life-span development.* (15th ed.). Boston: McGraw-Hill Publishers. NOTE: McGraw-Hill also offers an online resource to accompany this text- *Connect.*

Sigelman, C.K. & Rider, E.A. (2014). *Life-span human development* (8th ed.). Belmont, CA: Wadsworth Cengage Learning.

Web Links

https://www.verywell.com/what-is-sociocultural-theory-2795088

http://www.learning-theories.com/vygotskys-social-learning-theory.html

https://www.youtube.com/watch?v=k4mbavO96oM

http://www.simplypsychology.org/Zone-of-Proximal-Development.html

https://www.google.com/?gws_rd=ssl#q=vygotsky+ppt

Tips for Instructors

While students may easily learn rote facts about the theories, they can better learn application of the theories to life-span development through opportunities for application. Examples are provided in this chapter and with each chapter on the theories for exam items and assignments that can promote integration of theory to life.

Tips for Students

These theories of life-span development provide core understanding of why we live the way we live. To borrow a concept from health care, understanding involves identification of the evidence. As you apply a theory to your life or the life of someone else, think about what is the evidence that you or the other person is representing that facet of that theory.

Information-Processing Theory

Background on the Information-Processing Theory

This theory focuses on how cognitive development is based on increasing capacity for processing information as a person manipulates information, monitors the information, and creates strategy with the information. Santrock (2015) noted that Robert Siegler was a key figure in creation of this theory and presented thinking as the process of perceiving, encoding, representing, storing, and retrieving information. A core part of cognitive development was learning good strategies for processing information. Four key processes in this theory are Executive Attention, Sustained Attention, Short-Term Memory, and Executive Function. Santrock (2015) (p. 215) defines these as:

- Executive Attention - Involvement of action planning, allocation of attention to goals, error detection and compensation, monitoring progress on tasks, and dealing with novel or difficult circumstances. (p. 215)

- Sustained Attention – Focused and extended engagement with an object, task, event, or other aspect of the environment. (p. 215)

- Short-term Memory – The memory component in which individuals retain information for up to 30 seconds, assuming there is no rehearsal of the information. (p. 215) Information is then stored in Long-Term Memory for retrieval later to use as needed.

- Executive Function – An umbrella-like concept that consists of a number of higher-level cognitive processes linked to the development of the brain's prefrontal cortex. Executive function involves managing one's thoughts to engage in goal-directed behavior and seslf-control.

As with Vygotsky, this theory is not organized into specific stages.

Figure 2 Information Processing Theory Model

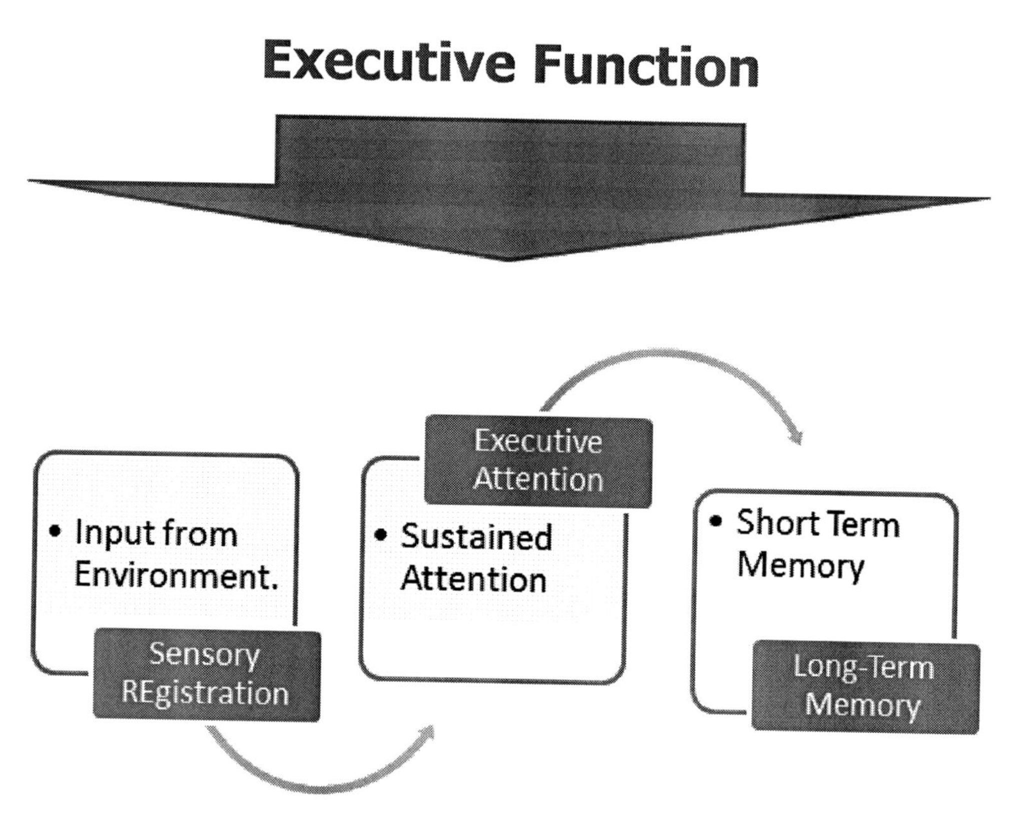

As a person receives input from his environment, he experiences **Sensory Regulation** in which the senses of sight, hearing, smell, taste, and touch provide information to the person. The person experiences **Sustained Attention** which grows into **Executive Attention** as the person acts on the information received. **Short Term Memory** facilitates thought and actions needed immediately. **Long Term Memory** retains the information for retrieval later in life as that information is needed again. These functions together comprise a person's **Executive Function.**

Exercises

1. Journaling – Begin a journal as you study the theories of lifespan development and write reflections about yourself for each theory and stage studied. For the Information Processing theory, describe what you remember about yourself over your development to this point in life that correlates with this theory.

2. Observation - Use your journal to take notes from observation of people who are currently in each of the life-span stages. As with yourself, note

how the person demonstrates application of the Information Processing Theory.

3. Research – Find a scholarly article on the Information Processing Theory and summarize that to share with your class. Focus on what the article teaches you about this theory and how you can apply that to your life and work.

4. Developmental Problems – Find information to share with your class on how each of the following conditions could cause significant challenges in development per this theory.
    a. A child who is born blind.
    b. A person who experiences amnesia after a severe automobile accident.
    c. A person who is diagnosed with Alzheimer's Disease.

5. Application to Life and Work – Reflect on application of the Information Processing Theory to your own life and work right now.
    a. How does the description of the stage you are in fit your own life now?
    b. How does this theory fit with the work that you do or that you plan to do?
    c. How does this theory fit with the significant other people in your life – family, best friends, co-workers, life partners, etc?

Case Study

Simon Says (or **Simple Simon Says**) is a child's game for 3 or more players where 1 player takes the role of "Simon" and issues instructions (usually physical actions such as "jump in the air" or "stick out your tongue") to the other players, which should only be followed if prefaced with the phrase "Simon says", for example, "Simon says, jump in the air". Players are eliminated from the game by either following instructions that are not immediately preceded by the phrase, or by failing to follow an instruction which does include the phrase "Simon says". It is the ability to distinguish between genuine and fake commands, rather than physical ability, that usually matters in the game; in most cases, the action just needs to be attempted.

The object for the player acting as Simon is to get all the other players out as quickly as possible; the winner of the game is usually the last player who has successfully followed all of the given commands. Occasionally however, 2 or more of the last players may all be eliminated by following a command without "Simon Says", thus resulting in Simon winning the game. (Retrieved from https://en.wikipedia.org/wiki/Simon_Says)

Reflection Questions

1. How does this game represent the following?
   - Executive Attention
   - Sustained Attention
   - Short-term Memory
   - Executive Function

2. Think of other games from childhood or even from sports and how these demonstrate the four processes of the Information-Processing Theory.

Practice Test Items

1. Describe the behavioral demonstration that you could observe in a person in each process of the Information - Processing theory.

2. Describe the communication that you could observe in a person in each process of the Information - Processing theory.

3. Describe some thoughts or thinking patterns that you could observe in a person in each process of the Information - Processing theory.

4. Describe what a parent or caregiver could do to help a child develop successfully through each process of the Information - Processing theory.

Additional Resources

Santrock, J. (2013). *Life-span development.* (15th ed.). Boston: McGraw-Hill Publishers. NOTE: McGraw-Hill also offers an online resource to accompany this text- *Connect.*

Sigelman, C.K. & Rider, E.A. (2014). *Life-span human development* (8th ed.). Belmont, CA: Wadsworth Cengage Learning.

Web Links

http://www.simplypsychology.org/information-processing.html

http://www.learning-theories.com/information-processing-theory.html

https://www.youtube.com/watch?v=pMMRE4Q2FGk

https://www.youtube.com/watch?v=GaucLgI9Hzo

https://www.google.com/?gws_rd=ssl#q=PPT+on+information+processing+theory+

Tips for Instructors

While students may easily learn rote facts about the theories, they can better learn application of the theories to life-span development through opportunities for application. Examples are provided in this chapter and with each chapter on the theories for exam items and assignments that can promote integration of theory to life.

Tips for Students

These theories of life-span development provide core understanding of why we live the way we live. To borrow a concept from health care, understanding involves identification of the evidence. As you apply a theory to your life or the life of someone else, think about what is the evidence that you or the other person is representing that facet of that theory.

Behavioral and Social Theories

Background

Behavioral and Social Theories focus on human development as observable behavior that reflects what a person is learning. This learning is through experience with the environment. These theories do not present development as sequential stages, but rather development as reflection of the continuity of learning from experience with the environment as exhibited in observable behavior.

Exercises

1. Compare and Contrast Essay/Paper

In one paragraph for each theory, describe the core construct of Skinner's theory and of Bandura's theory. Then provide a paragraph describing each of the following:

a. Strengths
   i. Bandura
   ii. Skinner
b. Weaknesses
   i. Bandura
   ii. Skinner
c. How Bandura's theory and Skinner's theory are alike
d. How Bandura's theory and Skinner's theory are different

2. Application for Today

Choose one of the following current issues of society and explain the difference in a Bandura view and a Skinner view of the issue.

a. Bullying of HS girl in bathroom
b. Pornography
c. School shooting
d. Discipline of parents or teachers with children
e. Religious standards

Practice Test Items

1. Compare and Contrast the theories of Bandura and Skinner on interaction of the person and the environment.

2. Explain how Bandura and Skinner each would explain how the following scenarios would work with Behavioral and Social Development in a 16 year old high school male.
    a. He gets suspended from the high school basketball team for three games for failure to show up to practice three times at the beginning of the season.
    b. He loses use of his cell-phone for two weeks for making a D on his report card.

3. Explain how Bandura and Skinner each would explain the role that television advertising has in the purchases that we make in our lives.

4. Explain how Bandura and Skinner each would explain the role that procrastination plays with a student who puts off a class project until the day before it is due.

Additional Resources

Textbooks

Santrock, J. (2013). *Life-span development*. (15th ed.). Boston: McGraw-Hill Publishers. NOTE: McGraw-Hill also offers an online resource to accompany this text- *Connect.*

Sigelman, C.K. & Rider, E.A.(2014). *Life-span human development* (8th ed.). Belmont, CA: Wadsworth Cengage Learning.

Web Links

https://www.verywell.com/child-development-theories-2795068

http://home.apu.edu/~ksetterlund/2012-2013/theories%20handout%20with%20terminology.pdf

http://www.richardsonthebrain.com/behavioral-theories/

https://www.youtube.com/watch?v=x7wZCtFWblE

https://www.google.com/?gws_rd=ssl#q=PPT+on+Behavioral+and+Social+theories

Tips for Instructors

While students may easily learn rote facts about the theories, they can better learn application of the theories to life-span development through opportunities for application. Examples are provided in this chapter and with each chapter on the theories for exam items and assignments that can promote integration of theory to life.

Tips for Students

These theories of life-span development provide core understanding of why we live the way we live. To borrow a concept from health care, understanding involves identification of the evidence. As you apply a theory to your life or the life of someone else, think about what is the evidence that you or the other person is representing that facet of that theory.

Bandura's Social Cognitive Theory

Background

Albert Bandura emphasized the mutual developmental influences of behavior, the person/cognition, and the environment. The person/cognition is represented through thinking, planning, and personal characteristics such as belief in one's capacity to control experiences. Bandura's theory proposes that relationships are reciprocal between behavior, the environment and the person/cognition. A core concept is this approach is observational learning in which a person develops from the influences from what he observes in others and then integrates these observed behaviors into his own life.

Figure 3 Bandura's Social Cognitive Model

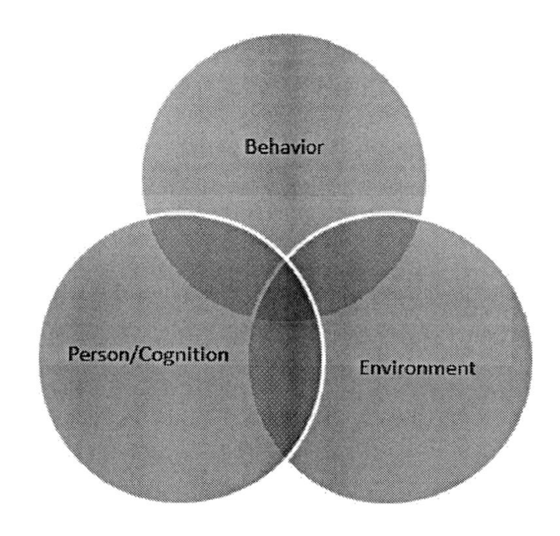

Exercises

1. Journaling – Begin a journal as you study the theories of lifespan development and write reflections about yourself for each theory and stage studied. For Bandura's theory, describe what you remember about yourself for each of the three components of this theory. Then reflect on how your memories correlate with the description of those components and your overall development to this point in your life..

2. Observation - Use your journal to take notes from observation of people who are currently in each of the life-span stages. As with yourself, note how the person demonstrates Bandura's theory in the three components.

3. Research – Find a scholarly article on Bandura's stages of life and summarize that to share with your class. Focus on what the article teaches you about Bandura's theory and how you can apply that to your life and work.

4. Developmental Problems – Bandura's theory emphasizes learning through observation and modeling. Discuss developmental challenges that could occur with each of the following situations.
   a. A kindergarten student whose mother constantly has different men friends over to do drugs and have sex several nights a week.
   b. A new college freshman who has never drunk any alcohol and now sees that almost every social event at college includes kegs of beer and almost everyone partakes of these freely.
   c. A 50 year old woman constantly sees television ads about coloring hair so that only her beautician will know about the gray, quick cosmetic surgery procedures to bring back her youth, and the *Good Housekeeping* Most Admired Women of the Year who all have done work very different from her status as a stay-at home mom and housekeeper for all of her adult life.

5. Application to Life and Work – Reflect on application of Bandura's theory to your own life and work right now.
   a. How does the description of the stage you are in fit your own life now?
   b. How does this theory fit with the work that you do or that you plan to do?
   c. How does this theory fit with the significant other people in your life – family, best friends, co-workers, life partners, etc?

Case Study

Joey is seven years old. He has an older brother who is on the high school basketball team and frequently practices with the basketball goal that that have set up by their garage and driveway. Johnny has started playing with the basketball also, trying the moves, throws, and spins that he has seen his older brother do. At home, Joey frequently sees his dad yelling in anger when he or his brother don't clean their room or do one of the other chores that are given to them by their parents. His dad often will put his finger right up in their face and threaten punishment as he yells at them. At school on the playground, Joey has begun to show the same behavior toward some of his classmates that he has seen in his dad.

Question for Reflection

Explain each of the following for Joey in his response to his observations of his brother and his response to his observation with his dad.

- Person/cognition
- Behavior
- Environment

Practice Test Items

1. Describe the behavioral demonstration that you could observe in a person in Bandura's theory.

2. Describe the communication that you could observe in a person in Bandura's theory.

3. Describe some thoughts or thinking patterns that you could observe in a person in Bandura's theory.

4. Describe what a parent or caregiver could do to help a child develop successfully through Bandura's theory.

Additional Resources

Textbooks

Santrock, J. (2013). *Life-span development.* (15th ed.). Boston: McGraw-Hill Publishers. NOTE: McGraw-Hill also offers an online resource to accompany this text- *Connect.*

Sigelman, C.K. & Rider, E.A. (2014). *Life-span human development* (8th ed.). Belmont, CA: Wadsworth Cengage Learning.

Web Links

http://www.learning-theories.com/social-learning-theory-bandura.html

https://www.youtube.com/watch?v=oyPNjYlboaw

https://www.youtube.com/watch?v=wf3-tRpmGmY

http://www.simplypsychology.org/bandura.html

https://www.google.com/?gws_rd=ssl#q=PPT+on+Bandura%27s+theory+

Tips for Instructors

While students may easily learn rote facts about the theories, they can better learn application of the theories to life-span development through opportunities for application. Examples are provided in this chapter and with each chapter on the theories for exam items and assignments that can promote integration of theory to life.

Tips for Students

These theories of life-span development provide core understanding of why we live the way we live. To borrow a concept from health care, understanding involves identification of the evidence. As you apply a theory to your life or the life of someone else, think about what is the evidence that you or the other person is representing that facet of that theory.

Skinner's Operant Conditioning

Background

B.F. Skinner is known for his work in Operant Conditioning, which is a process of behavioral formation in which the consequences of a behavior will influence the future probability of that behavior's occurrence. Rewards and punishments shape development through the influence of these stimuli on behavior. If a behavior is rewarded, it is more likely to recur in the future. If a behavior is punished, it is less likely to recur in the future. Patterns of behavior frame a person's overall development. The consequences of rewards or punishments for these behaviors continue to shape a person's life development.

Figure 4 Skinner's Operant Conditioning Model

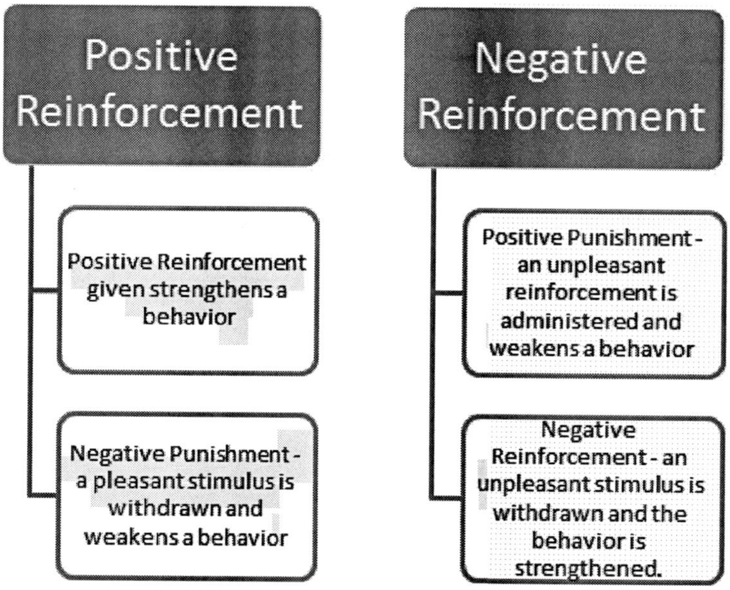

Positive Reinforcement
- Positive Reinforcement given strengthens a behavior
- Negative Punishment - a pleasant stimulus is withdrawn and weakens a behavior

Negative Reinforcement
- Positive Punishment - an unpleasant reinforcement is administered and weakens a behavior
- Negative Reinforcement - an unpleasant stimulus is withdrawn and the behavior is strengthened.

Exercises

1. Journaling – Begin a journal as you study the theories of lifespan development and write reflections about yourself for each theory and stage studied. For Skinner's theory, describe what you remember about yourself for the role of both reward and punishment throughout your life

2. Observation - Use your journal to take notes from observation of people who are currently in each of the life-span stages. As with yourself, note

how the person's life demonstrates the role of reward and punishment as influences on his or her development.

3. Research – Find a scholarly article on Skinner's stages of life and summarize that to share with your class. Focus on what the article teaches you about Skinner's theory and how you can apply that to your life and work.

4. Developmental Problems – Sometimes those in authority such as parents, teachers, or bosses complain that either the rewards they offer or the punishment they use does not seem to influence desired changes in behavior of those individuals under their authority. Study and reflect on this to determine why this could be a challenge and what modifications might be needed to facilitate more positive development for the individuals.

5. Application to Life and Work – Reflect on application of Skinner's theory to your own life and work right now.
   a. How does the description of the stage you are in fit your own life now?
   b. How does this theory fit with the work that you do or that you plan to do?
   c. How does this theory fit with the significant other people in your life – family, best friends, co-workers, life partners, etc?

Case Study

Sarah is a new teacher for third grade in a local elementary school. She knows that classroom management is going to be a key to her success. She found these classroom rules on the internet at http://www.3rdgradethoughts.com/2012/03/my-class-rules-printables.html and wants to try them in her classroom.

Rule #1: Listen when your teacher is talking.
Rule #2: Follow directions quickly.
Rule #3: Respect others , respect yourself , and respect your school .
Rule #4: Raise your hand to speak or stand .
Rule #5: Be safe, be kind , be honest .

Reflection Questions

1. Describe specific behavior you would want to see from a student for each rule to be followed.

2. If you were Sarah, for each rule, list a consequence that you could provide to fit each of the following.
    a. Positive Reinforcement
    b. Negative Reinforcement
    c. Positive Punishment
    d. Negative Punishment

Practice Test Items

1. Describe the behavioral demonstration that you could observe in a person in Skinner's Operant Conditioning theory.

2. Describe the communication that you could observe in a person in Skinner's Operant Conditioning theory.

3. Describe some thoughts or thinking patterns that you could observe in Skinner's Operant Conditioning theory.

4. Describe what a parent or caregiver could do to help a child develop successfully through Skinner's Operant Conditioning theory.

Additional Resources

Textbooks

Santrock, J. (2013). *Life-span development.* (15th ed.). Boston: McGraw-Hill Publishers. NOTE: McGraw-Hill also offers an online resource to accompany this text- *Connect.*

Sigelman, C.K. & Rider, E.A. (2014). *Life-span human development* (8th ed.). Belmont, CA: Wadsworth Cengage Learning.

Web Links

http://www.simplypsychology.org/operant-conditioning.html

http://www.learning-theories.com/operant-conditioning-skinner.html

https://www.google.com/?gws_rd=ssl#q=PPT+on+Skinner%27s+Operant+Conditioning+Theory

https://www.youtube.com/watch?v=ut1zmfolM9E

https://www.youtube.com/watch?v=kexFINXbJo4

Tips for Instructors

While students may easily learn rote facts about the theories, they can better learn application of the theories to life-span development through opportunities for application. Examples are provided in this chapter and with each chapter on the theories for exam items and assignments that can promote integration of theory to life.

Tips for Students

These theories of life-span development provide core understanding of why we live the way we live. To borrow a concept from health care, understanding involves identification of the evidence. As you apply a theory to your life or the life of someone else, think about what is the evidence that you or the other person is representing that facet of that theory.

Biological and Contextual Theories

Background

Biological and Contextual Theories expound further on the influences of nature and nurture in human development. These theories elaborate on the role of nature in development as development occurs from a person's organic, genetic inheritance as well as the environmental influences commonly considered to be the nurture side of influence in development.

Exercises

1. Compare and Contrast Essay/Paper

In one paragraph for each theory, describe the core construct of the Ecological Theory, the Ethological Theory, and Kohlberg's Theory of Moral Reasoning. Then provide a paragraph describing each of the following:

a. Strengths

i. Ecological Theory

ii. Ethological Theory

iii. Kohlberg's Theory of Moral Reasoning

b. Weaknesses

i. Ecological Theory

ii. Ethological Theory

ii. Kohlberg's Theory of Moral Reasoning

c. Commonalities among the Ecological, the Ethological and Kohlberg's theories.

d. Differences among the Ecological, the Ethological and Kohlberg's theories.

2. Application for Today

Choose one of the following current issues of society and explain the difference in how these scenarios would be explained per the Ecological, the Ethological and Kohlberg's theories.

a. Bullying of HS girl in bathroom

b. Pornography

c. School shooting

d. Politics

e. Religious standards

Practice Test Items

1. Describe the role of nature across the Ecological, Ethological, and Kohlberg theories.

2. Describe the role of nurture across the Ecological, Ethological, and Kohlberg theories.

3. Describe how the Ecological, Ethological, and Kohlberg theories would explain differences in development between a child in a third-world country that was constantly ravaged by war and a child living in the luxury of Martha's Vineyard.

4. Describe how the Ecological, Ethological, and Kohlberg theories would explain differences in development of a child growing up in an orphanage from birth and a child growing up in the home of his family of origin with his mother and father.

Additional Resources

Textbooks

Santrock, J. (2013). *Life-span development.* (15th ed.). Boston: McGraw-Hill Publishers. NOTE: McGraw-Hill also offers an online resource to accompany this text- *Connect.*

Sigelman, C.K. & Rider, E.A. (2014). *Life-span human development* (8th ed.). Belmont, CA: Wadsworth Cengage Learning.

Web Links

http://lrrpublic.cli.det.nsw.edu.au/lrrSecure/Sites/LRRView/7401/documents/theories_outline.pdf

https://sielearning.tafensw.edu.au/MCS/CHCFC301A/12048/chcfc301a/lo/12020/index.htm

http://www.gulfbend.org/poc/view_doc.php?&id=7924

http://hollich.psych.purdue.edu/235/Lecture1-Theories&Themes.pdf

http://highered.mheducation.com/sites/0072820144/student_view0/chapter1/index.html

Tips for Instructors

While students may easily learn rote facts about the theories, they can better learn application of the theories to life-span development through opportunities for application. Examples are provided in this chapter and with each chapter on the theories for exam items and assignments that can promote integration of theory to life.

Tips for Students

These theories of life-span development provide core understanding of why we live the way we live. To borrow a concept from health care, understanding involves identification of the evidence. As you apply a theory to your life or the life of someone else, think about what is the evidence that you or the other person is representing that facet of that theory.

Ecological Theory - Brofenbrenner

Background

Ecological Theory focuses on environmental influences on human development. Urie Bronfenbrenner proposed five environmental systems that influence development. The theory explains a range of contexts that provide developmental influence as well as connections between these systems.

Figure 5 Bronfenbrenner's Ecological Model

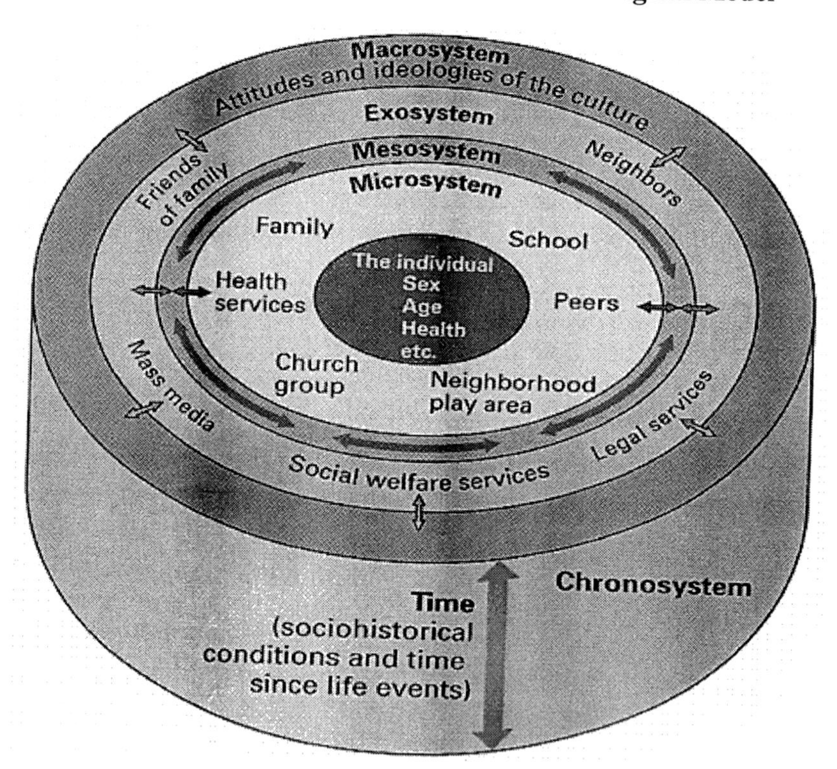

www.coursehero.com

Exercises

1. Journaling – Begin a journal as you study the theories of lifespan development and write reflections about yourself for each theory and stage studied. For the Ecological Theory, describe influences on your life to date from each of the five systems in this model.

2. Observation - Use your journal to take notes from observation of people who are currently in each of the life-span stages. As with yourself, note what influences are in their lives from each of the five systems of this model.

3. Research – Find a scholarly article on the Ecological Model and summarize that to share with your class. Focus on what the article teaches you about this theory and how you can apply that to your life and work.

4. Developmental Problems – Think about the following life challenges and how aspects of the respective systems contribute to the challenge and also how factors in a system could help to mediate the challenge.
   a. An elementary student who spends considerable time with In School Suspension.
   b. A 35 year old woman who consistently has to stay with her two young children at the local shelter for Domestic Violence.
   c. An 85 year widower who has been showing signs of Alzheimers Disease and whose son just took his car keys away from him and has plans to move him to a local nursing home.

5. Application to Life and Work – Reflect on application of the Ecological Theory to your own life and work right now.
   a. How does the description of the stage you are in fit your own life now?
   b. How does this theory fit with the work that you do or that you plan to do?
   c. How does this theory fit with the significant other people in your life – family, best friends, co-workers, life partners, etc?

Case Study

Santrock(2015) begins his text on Life-Span Development by sharing the following accounts of two different individuals (p. 3)

"Ted Kaczynski sprinted through high school, not bothering with his junior year and making only passing efforts at social contact. Off to Harvard at age 16, Kaczynski was a loner during his college years. One of his roommates at Harvard said the he avoided people by quickly shuffling by them and slamming the door behind him. After obtaining his PhD in mathematics at the University of Michigan, Kaczynski became a professor at the University of California at Berkeley. His colleagues there remember him as hiding from social contact – no friends, no allies, no networking.

After several years at Berkeley, Kaczynski resigned and moved to a rural area of Montanan where he lived as a hermit in a crude shack for 25 years. Town residents described him as a bearded eccentric. Kaczynski traced his own difficulties to growing up as a genius in a kid's body and sticking out like a sore thumb in his surroundings as a child. In 1996, he was arrested and charged as the notorious Unabomber, America's most wanted killer. Over the course of 17 years, Kaczynski had sent 16 mail bombs that left 23 people wounded or maimed and 3 people dead. In 1998, he pleaded guilty to the offenses and was sentenced to life in prison."

" A decade before Kaczynski mailed his first bomb, Alice Walker spent her days battling racism in Mississippi. She had recently won her first writing fellowship, but rather than use the money to follow her dream of moving to Senegai, Africa, she put herself into the heart and the heat of the civil rights movement. Walker had grown up knowing the brutal effects of poverty and racism. Born in 19444, she was the eighth child of Georgia sharecroppers who earned $300 a year. When Walker was 8 years old, her brother accidentally shot her in the left eye with a BB gun. By the time her parents got her to the hospital a week later (they had no car), she was blind in that eye, and it had developed a disfiguring layer of scar tissue. Despite the counts against her, Walker overcame pain and went on to win a Pulitzer Prize for her book **The Color Purple***. She became not only a novelist but also an essayist, a poet, a short-story writer, and a social activist."*

Reflection Question

Describe each of the systems below of the Ecological Theory as these apply to Ted Kaczynski and to Alice Walker.

- The Individual
- Microsystem
- Mesosystem
- Exosystem
- Macrosystem
- Chronosystem

Practice Test Items

1. Describe the behavioral demonstration that you could observe in a person in each system of the Ecological theory.

2. Describe the communication that you could observe in a person in each system of the Ecological theory.

3. Describe some thoughts or thinking patterns that you could observe in a person in each system of the Ecological theory.

4. Describe what a parent or caregiver could do to help a child develop successfully through each system of the Ecological theory.

Additional Resources

Textbooks

Santrock, J. (2013). *Life-span development.* (15th ed.). Boston: McGraw-Hill Publishers. NOTE: McGraw-Hill also offers an online resource to accompany this text- *Connect.*

Sigelman, C.K. & Rider, E.A. (2014). *Life-span human development* (8th ed.). Belmont, CA: Wadsworth Cengage Learning.

Web Links

http://www.psychologynoteshq.com/bronfenbrenner-ecological-theory/

http://study.com/academy/lesson/bronfenbrenners-ecological-systems-theory-of-development-definition-examples.html

https://www.mentalhelp.net/articles/urie-bronfenbrenner-and-child-development/

http://dropoutprevention.org/wp-content/uploads/2015/07/paquetteryanwebquest_20091110.pdf

https://www.youtube.com/watch?v=-n9WnqIMCjs

Tips for Instructors

While students may easily learn rote facts about the theories, they can better learn application of the theories to life-span development through opportunities for application. Examples are provided in this chapter and with each chapter on the theories for exam items and assignments that can promote integration of theory to life.

Tips for Students

These theories of life-span development provide core understanding of why we live the way we live. To borrow a concept from health care, understanding involves identification of the evidence. As you apply a theory to your life or the life of someone else, think about what is the evidence that you or the other person is representing that facet of that theory.

Ethological Theory

Background

The Ethological Theory focuses on the strong influences of biology and critical periods of development in life that can have long-lasting influence on a person. Ethology studies how species-specific behavior is adapted to support survival. Certain experiences early in life are considered crucial for life-long development, such as positive early attachment with a caregiver. This theory places value on observations in naturalistic settings. A key contributors to the theory were Konrad Lonrenz who conducted much research with imprinting grey lag geese. John Bowlby's theory on attachment also provided a key application of Ethological Theory.

Figure 6 Ethological Theoretical Model

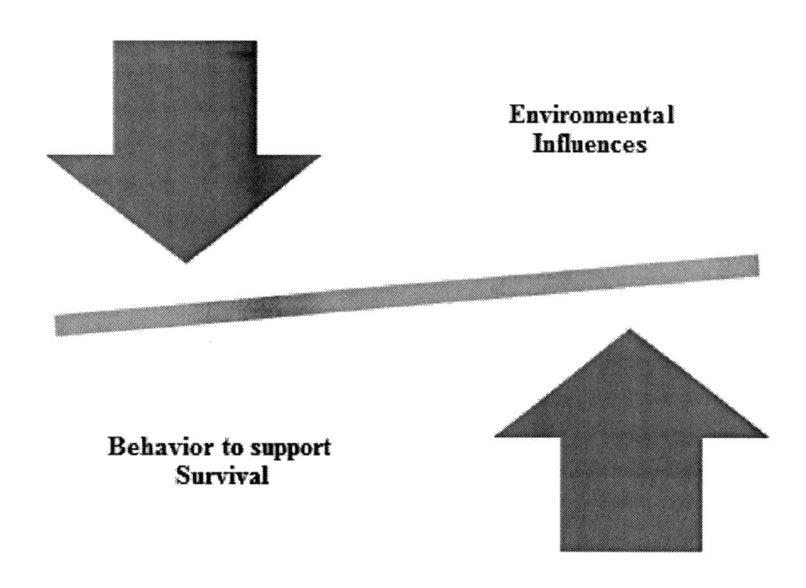

Exercises

1. Journaling – Begin a journal as you study the theories of lifespan development and write reflections about yourself for each theory and stage studies. For the ethological theory, describe early experiences that you had in life that had profound influence on your development – these may be experiences that you remember or that someone else has told you about. Also reflect on the relationship of John Bowlby's Attachment Theory to your own life.

2. Observation - Use your journal to take notes from observation of people

who are currently in each of the life-span stages and how early life experiences and Bowlby's Attachment Theory relate to them.

3. Research – Find a scholarly article on the Ethological Theory and summarize that to share with your class. Focus on what the article teaches you about this theory and how you can apply that to your life and work.

4. Developmental Problems – The Ethological Theory emphasizes the important developmental influence of imprinting by early life experiences. Early life experiences can be negative or positive. Reflect on possible influence of life development that could come from these experiences.
   a. A child is bitten by a neighbor's dog at the age of five.
   b. A four year old girl is sexually molested by her mother's boyfriend.
   c. A two year old accidentally gets burned by touching the space heater in the den.

5. Application to Life and Work – Reflect on application of the Ethological Theory to your own life and work right now.
   a. How does the description of the stage you are in fit your own life now?
   b. How does this theory fit with the work that you do or that you plan to do?
   c. How does this theory fit with the significant other people in your life – family, best friends, co-workers, life partners, etc?

Case Study

Suni is a two year old girl from China who has just been adopted by Caucasian parents in the United States. They enroll her in a local Day-Care program near their home and as she grow, they are very conscientious about giving Suni opportunities to socialize and learn from new culture – opportunities such as attendance at the local public school and participation in Girl Scouts, and their local church youth group.

The movie, *Dances with Wolves*, was about the relationship between a Civil War soldier and a band of Sioux Indians. The film opens on a particularly dark note, as melancholy Union lieutenant John W. Dunbar attempts to kill himself on a suicide mission, but instead becomes an unintentional hero. His actions lead to his reassignment to a remote post in remote South Dakota, where he encounters the Sioux. Attracted by the natural simplicity of their lifestyle, he chooses to leave his former life behind to join them, taking on the name Dances with Wolves. Soon, Dances with Wolves has become a welcome member of the tribe and fallen in love with a white woman who has been raised amongst the tribe. In the movie, the character Dances with Wolves lives as a Sioux with dress, behavior, habits, etc.

Reflection Questions

1. While neither of these cases involved the first year of life, some of the basic constructs of the Ethological Theory could still apply. Describe relationship between the Ethological Theory and each of these cases.

2. Describe the relationship of John Bowlby's Attachment Theory to each of these cases.

Practice Test Items

1. Describe the behavioral demonstration that you could observe in a person in the Ethological theory.

2. Describe the communication that you could observe in a person in the Ethological theory.

3. Describe some thoughts or thinking patterns that you could observe in a person in the Ethological theory.

4. Describe what a parent or caregiver could do to help a child develop successfully through the Ethological theory.

Additional Resources

Textbooks

Santrock, J. (2013). *Life-span development.* (15th ed.). Boston: McGraw-Hill Publishers. NOTE: McGraw-Hill also offers an online resource to accompany this text- *Connect.*

Sigelman, C.K. & Rider, E.A. 2014). *Life-span human development* (8th ed.).

Belmont, CA: Wadsworth Cengage Learning.

Woolfork, A. & Perry, N. (2015). *Child and adolescent development* (2nd ed.) Upper Saddle River, NJ: Pearson.

Web Links

http://study.com/academy/lesson/ethological-theory-definition-lesson-quiz.html

http://what-when-how.com/child-development/ethological-theories-child-development/

https://www.youtube.com/watch?v=Gm-_xx7-Xec

http://virtual-lecture-hall.com/KRA2605cssCHAPTER2/etho.html

https://prezi.com/vzg9suwugtvf/ethological-vs-ecological-development/

Tips for Instructors

While students may easily learn rote facts about the theories, they can better learn application of the theories to life-span development through opportunities for application. Examples are provided in this chapter and with each chapter on the theories for exam items and assignments that can promote integration of theory to life.

Tips for Students

These theories of life-span development provide core understanding of why we live the way we live. To borrow a concept from health care, understanding involves identification of the evidence. As you apply a theory to your life or the life of someone else, think about what is the evidence that you or the other person is representing that facet of that theory.

Kohlberg

Background

Lawrence Kohlberg presented six stages of universal moral development. His theory is included as a contextual theory in that moral development is framed by reasoning and interaction between the person and the context in which lived. As a person develops through this model, moral reasoning becomes more internalized. Kohlberg proposed that development moved across these stages as a person had opportunity to take the perspective of another person and reflect on the conflict between his or her current stage of moral reasoning and that of a person at a higher level of moral reasoning. While development per stages tends to occur at age levels as depicted below, in general must children have pre-conventional morality and most adults have conventional morality. Kohlberg's estimate was that only 20 to 25 percent of the population ever attains the post-conventional level of morality.

Table 5 Kohlberg's Model of Moral Reasoning – Levels and Stages

Level		Stages in Level		Typical Age Range
1	**Pre-conventional Reasoning** This is the lowest level of moral reasoning in which the person has no internalization of morality and moral reasoning is governed by rewards and punishments.	**Stage 1** **Heteronomous Morality**	Moral thinking is tied to the consequence of punishment. Rules are obeyed to avoid punishment.	2 to 6 years.
		Stage 2 **Individualism, instrumental purpose, and exchange**	Individuals focus on own interests, but allow for others to do the same. The choice to act positively toward another person is related to an expectation that this will prompt the other person to also act positively toward the individual.	5 to 7 years

2	**Conventional Reasoning** Individuals abide by internalized standards that they have received from others, such as parents or laws of society.	Stage 3 **Mutual interpersonal expectations, relationships, and interpersonal conformity.**	Individuals base moral reasoning on trust, caring, and loyalty to others.	7 to 12 years
		Stage 4 **Social System Morality**	Individuals base moral reasoning on their understanding of social order, law, justice, and duty.	10 to 5 years
3	**Post Conventional Reasoning** Individuals abide by an internal personal moral code that has developed from recognition of choices, exploration of the choices, and decision on a choice.	Stage 5 **Social contract or utility and individual rights**	Individuals reason that the law is based on values, rights and principles. There is examination and evaluation of social systems for degree to which basic human rights are protected and valued.	Could start as early as 12
		Stage 6 **Universal Ethical Principles**	The individual follows a personal moral standard that is based on universal human rights. When faced with a conflict between the law and individual conscience, the individual will follow conscience, even if this decision includes potential of personal risk.	

Exercises

1. Journaling – Begin a journal as you study the theories of lifespan development and write reflections about yourself for each theory and stage studied. For Kohlberg's theory, describe what you remember about yourself for each of the stages of this theory. Then reflect on how your memories correlate with the description of that stage of Kohlberg's theory.

2. Observation - Use your journal to take notes from observation of people who are currently in each of the stages of Kohlberg's theory. As with yourself, note how the person demonstrates the applicable stage or not.

3. Research – Find a scholarly article on Kohlberg's stages of life and summarize that to share with your class. Focus on what the article teaches you about Kohlberg's theory and how you can apply that to your life and work.

4. Developmental Problems –
   a. While Kohlberg estimated certain age ranges for the development of the stages of his theory, he also noted that the stage of Social Contracts/Utility and Individual Rights could start as early as age 12. Reflect on life influences that might provide for a 12 year old to have that level of moral reasoning.
   b. Kohlberg noted that only 20 to 25 percent of the population would ever reach the stage of Universal Rights. Reflect on why most of us would never reach that stage and also reflect on what life influences might lead a person to reach stage 6.

5. Application to Life and Work – Reflect on application of Kohlberg's theory to your own life and work right now.
   a. How does the description of the stage you are in fit your own life now?
   b. How does this theory fit with the work that you do or that you plan to do?
   c. How does this theory fit with the significant other people in your life – family, best friends, co-workers, life partners, etc?

Case Study

Kevin is a United States Marine on Patrol in a war zone in the Middle-East. He steps around the corner of a building and immediately faces a man whom he recognizes as an enemy soldier, because of his uniform. The man is unarmed and is clutching his side where the uniform appears to be bloody.

Reflection Question

Reflect on possible thoughts that Kevin could have and possible courses of action that he could take. Describe what these might be at each of the six stages of Kohlberg's theory.

1. Heteronomous morality
2. Individualism, instrumental purpose, and exchange
3. Mutual interpersonal expectations, relationships, and exchange
4. Social systems morality
5. Social contract or utility and individual rights
6. Universal ethical principles

Practice Test Items

1. Describe the behavioral demonstration that you could observe in a person in each level and stage of Kohlberg's theory.

2. Describe the communication that you could observe in a person in each level and stage of Kohlberg's theory.

3. Describe some thoughts or thinking patterns that you could observe in a person in each level and stage of Kohlberg's theory.

4. Describe what a parent or caregiver could do to help a child develop successfully through each level and stage of Kohlberg's theory.

Additional Resources

Textbooks

Santrock, J. (2013). *Life-span development*. (15th ed.). Boston: McGraw-Hill Publishers. NOTE: McGraw-Hill also offers an online resource to accompany this text- *Connect.*

Sigelman, C.K. & Rider, E.A. (2014). *Life-span human development* (8th ed.). Belmont, CA: Wadsworth Cengage Learning.

Web links

http://thebrain.mcgill.ca/flash/i/i_09/i_09_s/i_09_s_dev/i_09_s_dev.html

http://www.simplypsychology.org/kohlberg.html

http://pegasus.cc.ucf.edu/~ncoverst/Kohlberg's%20Stages%20of%20Moral%20Development.htm

http://www.psychologynoteshq.com/kohlbergstheory/

https://www.youtube.com/watch?v=Onkd8tChC2A

Tips for Instructors

While students may easily learn rote facts about the theories, they can better learn application of the theories to life-span development through opportunities for application. Examples are provided in this chapter and with each chapter on the theories for exam items and assignments that can promote integration of theory to life.

Tips for Students

These theories of life-span development provide core understanding of why we live the way we live. To borrow a concept from health care, understanding involves identification of the evidence. As you apply a theory to your life or the life of someone else, think about what is the evidence that you or the other person is representing that facet of that theory.

Theories Relevant to Later Life

Background

Late Adulthood is the last stage of the life-span. While all of the previously discussed theories have application to later life, there are two theories that focus on facets of life development that tend to be most experienced in this last stage of life. The first theory focuses on developmental experiences with social relationships, emotional health, and knowledge. The second theory focuses on the process of death or loss. While death and loss do occur at all ages of life, this is seen more by those in later life as they live out a life-span that fits the typical number of years for mankind to live.

Exercises

1. Compare and Contrast Essay/Paper

In one paragraph for each theory, describe the core construct of the Socioemotional Selectivity Theory and of the Kubler-Ross Model. Then provide a paragraph describing each of the following:

a. Strengths

  i. Socioemotional Selectivity

  ii. Kubler-Ross

b. Weaknesses

  i. Socioemotional Selectivity

  ii Kubler-Ross

2. Application for Today

a. Do some research and reflect on how the Socioemotional Selectivity Theory and the Kubler-Ross Model might apply differently per these scenarios.

  i. An African American family in Alabama who are actively involved in their local Baptist church.

  ii. Mother Teresa (if she were still living)

  iii. A wealthy Caucasian family from New Jersey with a 75 year old man (head of the household) serving as a U.S. Senator from that state.

Practice Test Items

1. Describe commonalities in consideration of development from the Socioemotional Selectivity theory and the Kubler-Ross Model of Grief.

2. Describe differences a person might have in their relationships with family and community associates according to the Socioemotional Selectivity Theory and the Kubler-Ross Model of Grief.

3. Describe the role that a person's spirituality might have in the Socioemotional Selectivity Theory and the Kubler-Ross Model of Grief.

4. Describe the role that a person's culture might have in the Socioemotional Selectivity Theory and the Kubler-Ross Model of Grief.

Additional Resources

Textbooks

Santrock, J. (2013). *Life-span development*. (15th ed.). Boston: McGraw-Hill Publishers. NOTE: McGraw-Hill also offers an online resource to accompany this text- *Connect.*

Sigelman, C.K. & Rider, E.A. (2014). *Life-span human development* (8th ed.). Belmont, CA: Wadsworth Cengage Learning.

Web Links

https://www.cliffsnotes.com/study-guides/psychology/psychology/developmental-psychology-age-13-to-65/development-in-late-adulthood

http://study.com/academy/topic/psychosocial-and-cognitive-development-in-late-adulthood.html

https://prezi.com/g78h4kbpkrgi/late-adulthood-emotional-and-social-development/

https://www.youtube.com/watch?v=pV4lKyEgr4Y

https://www.youtube.com/watch?v=rvglD4tVawk

Tips for Instructors

While students may easily learn rote facts about the theories, they can better learn application of the theories to life-span development through opportunities for application. Examples are provided in this chapter and with each chapter on the theories for exam items and assignments that can promote integration of theory to life.

Tips for Students

These theories of life-span development provide core understanding of why we live the way we live. To borrow a concept from health care, understanding involves identification of the evidence. As you apply a theory to your life or the life of someone else, think about what is the evidence that you or the other person is representing that facet of that theory.

Socioemotional Selectivity Theory

Background

Laura Carstensen developed a theory that focus on the social and emotional development of older adults. She proposed that as people age, they place a high value on emotional satisfaction and devote more time to those relationships which are more rewarding for them. At the same time, they lessen interaction with individuals who have just peripheral social contact with them. This theory also emphasizes the two types of goals for older adults – knowledge-related and emotional. As people become aware of having less future time in their lives, more time is spent in pursuit of quality emotional satisfaction and less time in pursuit of information.

Figure 7 Socioemotional Selectivity Theory Model Projectory

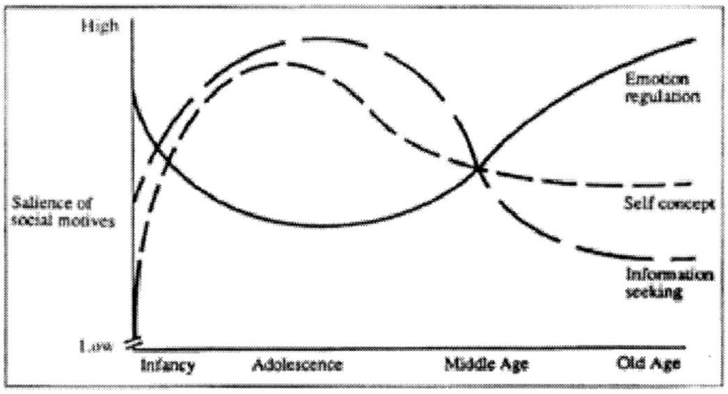

www.dep6059.wikispaces.com

Exercises

1. Journaling – Begin a journal as you study the theories of lifespan development and write reflections about yourself for each theory and stage studied. For the Socioemotional Selectivity theory, describe how this either does or might apply to you as you experience your middle adulthood years.

2. Observation - Use your journal to take notes from observation of people who are currently in Middle Adulthood and Late Adulthood. As with yourself, note how the person demonstrates this theory or not.

3. Research – Find a scholarly article on the Socioemotional Selectivity Theory and summarize that to share with your class. Focus on what

the article teaches you about this theory and how you can apply that to your life and work.

4. Developmental Problems – Reflect on benefits and disadvantages a person might have as their life begins to align with the Socioemotional Selectivity Theory.

5. Application to Life and Work – Reflect on application of the Socioemotional Selectivity theory to your own life and work right now.
   a. How does the description of the stage you are in fit your own life now?
   b. How does this theory fit with the work that you do or that you plan to do?
   c. How does this theory fit with the significant other people in your life – family, best friends, co-workers, life partners, etc?

Case Study

Mr. Jones recently retired as a supervisor for one section of a local manufacturing company. He lives with his wife of 40 years and their son and daughter live in the same town, each within a 15 minute drive from Mr. Jones and his wife. Their son has two children at home and their daughter has one child still at home. Mr. Jones has been active in several local civic organizations and with his companies various volunteer projects in the community. As Mr. Jones gives his speech at the company retirement ceremony, he says, "I have enjoyed working with all of you, playing ball with the team, and helping our community with the various goodwill projects that we have. But, I will be honest with you, as I retire, I plan to spend a lot more time with my wife on vacations, with my grandkids, and building odd and end things in my woodshop behind our house."

Reflection Question

Describe how Mr. Jones planned transition from retirement relates to the Socioemotional Selectivity Theory.

Practice Test Items

1. Describe the behavioral demonstration that you could observe in a person in the Socioemotional Selectivity theory.

2. Describe the communication that you could observe in a person in the Socioemotional Selectivity theory.

3. Describe some thoughts or thinking patterns that you could observe in a person in the Socioemotional Selectivity theory.

4. Describe what a child or caregiver could do to help a older adult develop successfully through the Socioemotional Selectivity theory.

Additional Resources

Textbooks

Santrock, J. (2013). *Life-span development.* (15th ed.). Boston: McGraw-Hill Publishers. NOTE: McGraw-Hill also offers an online resource to accompany this text- *Connect.*

Sigelman, C.K. & Rider, E.A. (2014). *Life-span human development* (8th ed.). Belmont, CA: Wadsworth Cengage Learning.

Web Links

https://sites.google.com/site/socioemotionalselectivetheory/history-of-socioemotional-selectivity-theory

http://www.ted.com/talks/laura_carstensen_older_people_are_happier?language=en

http://www.ncbi.nlm.nih.gov/pubmed/25984789

http://www.psychwiki.com/wiki/PSY323-Socioemotional_Selectivity_Theory

https://www.youtube.com/watch?v=ZrHGPv9G-AQ

Tips for Instructors

While students may easily learn rote facts about the theories, they can better learn application of the theories to life-span development through opportunities for application. Examples are provided in this chapter and with each chapter on the theories for exam items and assignments that can promote integration of theory to life.

Tips for Students

These theories of life-span development provide core understanding of why we live the way we live. To borrow a concept from health care, understanding involves identification of the evidence. As you apply a theory to your life or the life of someone else, think about what is the evidence that you or the other person is representing that facet of that theory.

Kubler-Ross Theory of Grief

Background

Elisabeth Kubler-Ross provided a model of the stages/reactions with death and dying. According to this model, a dying person as well as those close to him or her go through five developmental stages in dealing with the death. This model can also be applied to other life experiences of loss.

Table 8 Kubler-Ross Stages of Dying and Grief

Stage/Reaction	Description of Stage
Denial and Isolation	The individual denies the death or loss.
Anger	The individual accepts the presence of the death or loss and responds with feelings of anger, resentment, rage, or envy. Anger may be project toward caregivers, medical personnel, or even God. The anger may be especially directed toward those who symbolize vibrant life to the person.
Bargaining	The individual develops a hope that the death or loss might be postponed. The individual may desire a longer time before the finalization of the loss in exchange for accomplishment of some goal.
Depression	The individual accepts the inevitability of the loss with demonstration of some depression or preparatory grief. This is an effort of the individual to distance self from objects of love and contemplate the final death of finalization of other loss.
Acceptance	In this final stage, the individual develops a sense of peace with acceptance of his or her fate. Often there is a desire to be left alone and there may be greatly diminished feelings or physical pain.

Exercises

1. Journaling – Begin a journal as you study the theories of lifespan development and write reflections about yourself for each theory and stage studies. For the Kubler-Ross Model, describe how this model has fit you with any loss that you have experienced in life, such as death of someone close to you or a pet, loss of a personal relationship such as a divorce or "breaking up" with a significant other friend or loss of a job.

2. Observation - Use your journal to take notes from observation of some other people you know and their experiences also as reflective of this model or not..

3. Research – Find a scholarly article on the Kubler-Ross Model and summarize that to share with your class. Focus on what the article teaches you about Freud's theory and how you can apply that to your life and work.

4. Developmental Problems – People who experience a loss in their lives can progress from Denial to Acceptance at different spans of time and in different ways. Reflect on challenges that could happen if a person got stuck in one of the stages of this model.

5. Application to Life and Work – Reflect on application of the Kubler-Ross Model to your own life and work right now.
    a. How does the description of this model fit your own life now?
    b. How does this model fit with the work that you do or that you plan to do?
    c. How does this model fit with the significant other people in your life – family, best friends, co-workers, life partners, etc?

Case Study

Mr. and Mrs. Taylor had one son, Marcus, who wanted to go into the United States Air Force when he graduated from high school. His mother was adamantly opposed to this as she was.afraid he might get hurt or killed in military action somewhere. Marcus yielded to his mother's wishes and got a job working with an oil well drilling crew instead. His job was to help with pipe drilling as new wells were being established. He had been working in this job for a couple of years and was engaged to be married in three months. One day while working on a rig, the casing at the top of the pipe being drilled into the ground slipped and fell on Marcus from a height of 50 feet. He was killed immediately.

Mr. and Mrs. Taylor had always been very active in their local church, always attending every service and every function that took place at the church. Mr. Taylor was known to have a keen sense of humor and was known to tell jokes and enjoy laughing with other people in the community. After Marcus was killed, Mrs. Taylor continued to live her life much as she always had – a homemaker who enjoyed visiting with neighbors and doing most of her shopping in the local town. Mr. Taylor immediately resigned from all of his responsibilities in the church and quite going to the church or any other church for any reason. He no longer got outside of his home much and never seemed to laugh anymore. 10 years after Marcus died, Mr. Taylor was diagnosed with lung cancer. A year after the diagnosis, one day he called the local Para-Medic and Ambulance company and said this, "You need to come out to my house and get me. You will find me in the shed behind the house." When the ambulance arrived at the house, they did find Mr. Taylor in the shed behind the house – dead with his shotgun lying beside him.

Reflection Question

Describe how each stage of the Kubler-Ross model seemed to apply to both Mr. Taylor and Mrs. Taylor.

Practice Test Items

1. Describe the behavioral demonstration that you could observe in a person in each stage of the Kubler-Ross model.
2. Describe the communication that you could observe in a person in each stage of the Kubler-Ross model.
3. Describe some thoughts or thinking patterns that you could observe in a person in each stage of the Kubler-Ross model.
4. Describe what a friend or family member could do to help a person who was grieving to develop successfully through each stage of the Kubler-Ross model.

Additional Resources

Textbooks

Santrock, J. (2013). *Life-span development.* (15th ed.). Boston: McGraw-Hill Publishers. NOTE: McGraw-Hill also offers an online resource to accompany this text- *Connect.*

Sigelman, C.K. & Rider, E.A. (2014). *Life-span human development* (8th ed.). Belmont, CA: Wadsworth Cengage Learning.

Web Links

http://www.amhc.org/58-grief-bereavement-issues/article/8444-stage-of-grief-models-kubler-ross

http://www.toolshero.com/change-management/five-stages-of-loss-and-grief-kubler/

http://www.change-management-coach.com/kubler-ross.html

http://grief.com/the-five-stages-of-grief/

https://www.youtube.com/watch?v=jTxOiq3V7Bw

Tips for Instructors

While students may easily learn rote facts about the theories, they can better learn application of the theories to life-span development through opportunities for application. Examples are provided in this chapter and with each chapter on the theories for exam items and assignments that can promote integration of theory to life.

Tips for Students

These theories of life-span development provide core understanding of why we live the way we live. To borrow a concept from health care, understanding involves identification of the evidence. As you apply a theory to your life or the life of someone else, think about what is the evidence that you or the other person is representing that facet of that theory.

Summary of Theories of Life-Span Development

Why We Live the Way We Live

The following table provides an overview of theoretical explanation of areas of life development. While theories may offer explanation across multiple life development areas, the key focus is shared in this table.

Table 9 Summary of Theories and Life Development Areas

Theory & Life Development Areas	Cognitive	Social	Moral	Physical	Contextual
Freud	Role of Ego	Sexual Drive motivation for behavior	Role of Super Ego	Influence of Inner Drives	Conflicts between inner drives and contextual expectations
Erikson	Decision making with crises	Primary motivation for development	Crisis resolution can influence moral decisions	Physical behaviors demonstrate response to crisis of stage.	Context influences management of each crisis and stage
Piaget	4 stages of cognitive development		Capacity for moral decision making and action with later stages of development	Behavioral development to carry out cognitive processing	Interaction with context as mature across stages
Vygotsky	Based on social and cultural influences	Supports learning via interactions with social world and culture	Moral reasoning influenced by social interactions and the culture of an individual	Behavior mirrors influence of social interactions and the culture of an individual.	Social and cultural context integrate with and frame learning

Information-Processing	Mental Management of Information through manipulation, monitoring, and creation of strategy	Receives input from social interactions	Makes moral decisions through processing information	Brain involvement in information processing.	Context provides input for information processing and is recipient of distribution of output.
Skinner	Cognitive processing to dictate response to consequences	Input of others to influence consequences of behavior	Input of others to influence consequences of behavior	Behavioral response patterns frame development.	Consequences of behavior connect with life contexts
Bandura	Learning through observation	Modeling behavior of others	Observations influence moral decisions	Observations influence physical behaviors	Influences learning and is recipient of behavior.
Ethological	Strong learning from imprinting in critical early stages of life	Strong influence of social imprinting early in life by key others	Early experiences can frame life-long moral decisions	Behavioral consequences exhibited per behavior.	Much use of observations in naturalistic settings.
Ecological	Cognitive processing of input from contexts	Contexts included various levels of stimulation for social development	Moral development to fit personal contexts	Contextual stimulation and modeling for physical development	Five environmental systems of influence
Kohlberg	Cognitive processing of moral decision making	Consideration and comparison of one's own moral reasoning and that of others	Focus of development is moral decision making across the life-span	Behavioral demonstration of moral reasoning.	Moral reasoning is both influenced by and acts on life contexts.

Socioemotional Selectivity	Less focus on knowledge acquisition	Focus on fewer and high quality relationships	Reasoning to support emotional satisfaction and others in quality relationships	Behavioral manifestations to reinforce emotional satisfaction with quality relationships	Interaction with contest is selective – focus on quality versus quantity
Kubler-Ross	Cognitive processing of each stage of model	Differences in social relationships per stage of model	Moral reasoning across stages of model	Behavioral demonstration of stages of model	Both input from and action toward life contexts across stages of model

CHAPTER 3

Areas of Personal Development

Background

Each person has multiple components of self in which he or she develops. These components are integrated into the whole person. All do not develop at the same rate through each lifespan stage. However course textbooks on lifespan development do provide norms for development to expect at each lifespan stage. When one of these components is not aligned well with the development in other components, there can be challenge to whole person functioning. The focus of this section is on the following areas of individual development.

Cognitive Development involves growth in a person's thought, intelligence and language. This development is evidenced by getting the most out of life by asking questions, being open to new ideas, learning new skills, and studying effectively.

Emotional Development involves growth in understanding one's own emotions and the emotions of others. This development also involves growth in self-regulation of emotions and growth in facets of emotional well-being such as self-esteem, self-confidence, optimism, and satisfaction in relationships.

Moral Development involves growth in a person's understanding and actions with rules and expectations on what should be done as people interact with each other.

Physical Development involves growth and functioning of our bodies. This development is reflected through maintaining optimal health by getting enough sleep, eating healthy, exercising, and avoiding unhealthy habits. It can also be reflected through practice of negative health habits such as negligence of one's body or practice of habits that are harmful to one's physical health.

Social Development involves growth and functioning of our relationships and interactions with other people. This development is evidenced in the quality and extent of supportive social networks, personal contributions to society, and treatment of cultural diversity.

Cultural Development involves growth and functioning within "shared values, beliefs, expectations, worldview, symbols, and appropriate learned behaviors of a group that provide its members with norms, plans, traditions, and rules for social living." (Gladding, 2011, p. 44)

Exercises

1. Using the definitions of the six areas of personal development, write about your own development to this point in your life by describing the successes and the challenges for you to date in each of the six areas.

2. Using the definitions of the six areas of personal development, create a Pecha Kucha (20 by 20) Power Point Presentation on yourself that shares your development in each of the six areas. While this exercise is similar to number 1, it will prompt you to use pictures and symbols to represent yourself versus just words. The Pecha Kuch format can be found at https://www.youtube.com/watch?v=YGVCKCn6jBc. This site provides more information on the benefit of using the Pecha Kucha format. http://www.usc.edu/dept/education/CMMR/Pecha_Kucha_TipsResourcesExamples.pdf

3. Application for today – Write a short essay reflecting on how the six areas can impact on a person's development in that setting. Consider all of life development to that point in that person's life.
   a. A child who is a member of the British royal family.
   b. A child who lives in inner city Bronx, New York.
   c. A child living on a farm in northwest Mississippi.
   d. An 88 year old woman with Alzheimer's living in a local nursing home.
   e. A 44 year-old man incarcerated in the state prison for vehicular homicide and this is his 12th year in prison.

Note on Case Studies for Section III. Case studies are not included in the chapters of Section III as the case studies in Section IV include each of the personal areas of development.

Practice Test Items

1. Describe how cognitive, emotional, and physical development could influence each other in the life of an adolescent female.

2. Describe how cognitive, emotional, and physical development could influence each other in the life of an older adult male who just retired from a job as a game warden.

3. Describe how moral, social, and cultural development could influence each other in the life of a female college student from China attending a small regional university in central Alabama.

4. Describe how moral, social, and cultural development could influence each other in the life of nine year old boy from the United States (Midwestern state) living with his Southern Baptist missionary parents in Thailand.

Additional Resources

Textbooks

Santrock, J. (2013). *Life-span development.* (15th ed.). Boston: McGraw-Hill Publishers. NOTE: McGraw-Hill also offers an online resource to accompany this text- *Connect.*

Sigelman, C.K. & Rider, E.A. (2014). *Life-span human development* (8th ed.). Belmont, CA: Wadsworth Cengage Learning.

Woolfolk, A. & Perry, N.E. (2015). *Child and Adolescent Development* (2nd ed.). Upper Saddle River, NJ: Pearson.

Web Links

http://personalgrowthmap.com/blog/2009/03/20/understanding-the-seven-life-areas/

http://cte.sfasu.edu/wp-content/uploads/2013/02/Four-Areas-of-Development-Preschool-to-School-Age-PPT.pdf

http://www.answers.com/Q/What_are_the_five_areas_of_development_in_children

http://www.icanteachmychild.com/domains-of-early-childhood-development/

http://befriendingyourbody.com/the-8-key-components-of-personal-wellness/

Tips for Instructors

While students may easily learn rote facts about the theories, they can better learn application of the theories to life-span development through opportunities for application. Examples are provided in this chapter and with each chapter on the theories for exam items and assignments that can promote integration of theory to life.

Tips for Students

These theories of life-span development provide core understanding of why we live the way we live. To borrow a concept from health care, understanding involves identification of the evidence. As you apply a theory to your life or the life of someone else, think about what is the evidence that you or the other person is representing that facet of that theory.

Cognitive

Background

Cognitive Development involves growth in a person's thought, intelligence and language. This development is evidenced by getting the most out of life by asking questions, being open to new ideas, learning new skills, and studying effectively.

Exercises

1. Journaling – Begin a journal as you studies the theories and areas of lifespan development and write reflections about yourself for each studied. For Cognitive development, describe what you remember about yourself about this area of development.

2. Observation - Use your journal to take notes from observation of several people whom you know well, such as family, friends, or co-workers. As with yourself, note how the person demonstrates his or her Cognitive development.

3. Research – Find a scholarly article on Cognitive development and summarize that to share with your class. Focus on what the article teaches you about Cognitive development and how you can apply that to your life and work.

4. Developmental Problems – As with most theories and areas of personal development, there is a normal way a person will develop. Identify examples of a person having other than normal Cognitive development and factors that could contribute to that from the perspectives of both nature and nurture.

5. Application to Life and Work – Reflect on application of personal Cognitive development to your own life and work right now.
   a. How does the description of normal Cognitive development fit your own life now?
   b. How does the description of normal Cognitive development fit with the work that you do or that you plan to do?
   c. How does this the description of normal Cognitive development fit with the significant other people in your life – family, best friends, co-workers, life partners, etc?

Practice Test Items

1. Describe Cognitive development from birth to age six.
   a. Normal development
   b. Some dysfunctional development issues that can occur during this time of life.

2. Describe Cognitive development from age six to age 11.
   a. Normal development
   b. Some dysfunctional development issues that can occur during this time of life.

3. Describe Cognitive development from age 12 to age 18.
   a. Normal development
   b. Some dysfunctional development issues that can occur during this time of life.

4. Describe Cognitive development during Early and Middle Adulthood.
   a. Normal development
   b. Some dysfunctional development issues that can occur during this time of life.

5. Describe Cognitive development during Late Adulthood.
   a. Normal development
   b. Some dysfunctional development issues that can occur during this time of life.

Additional Resources

Textbooks

Santrock, J. (2013). *Life-span development*. (15th ed.). Boston: McGraw-Hill Publishers. NOTE: McGraw-Hill also offers an online resource to accompany this text- *Connect.*

Sigelman, C.K. & Rider, E.A. (2014). *Life-span human development* (8th ed.). Belmont, CA: Wadsworth Cengage Learning.

Woolfolk, A. & Perry, N.E. (2015). *Child and Adolescent Development* (2nd ed.). Upper Saddle River, NJ: Pearson.

Web Links

https://www.cincinnatichildrens.org/health/c/cognitive

http://www.healthofchildren.com/C/Cognitive-Development.html

http://www.stanfordchildrens.org/en/topic/default?id=cognitive-development-90-P01594

http://study.com/academy/lesson/cognitive-development-in-adults.html

http://study.com/academy/lesson/cognitive-development-in-late-adulthood.html

Tips for Instructors

While students may easily learn rote facts about the theories, they can better learn application of the theories to life-span development through opportunities for application. Examples are provided in this chapter and with each chapter on the theories for exam items and assignments that can promote integration of theory to life.

Tips for Students

These theories of life-span development provide core understanding of why we live the way we live. To borrow a concept from health care, understanding involves identification of the evidence. As you apply a theory to your life or the life of someone else, think about what is the evidence that you or the other person is representing that facet of that theory.

Emotional

Background

Emotional Development involves growth in understanding one's own emotions and the emotions of others. This development also involves growth in self-regulation of emotions and growth in facets of emotional well-being such as self-esteem, self-confidence, optimism, and satisfaction in relationships.

Exercises

1. Journaling – Begin a journal as you studies the theories and areas of lifespan development and write reflections about yourself for each studied. For Emotional development, describe what you remember about yourself about this area of development.

2. Observation - Use your journal to take notes from observation of several people whom you know well, such as family, friends, or co-workers. As with yourself, note how the person demonstrates his or her Emotional development.

3. Research – Find a scholarly article on Emotional development and summarize that to share with your class. Focus on what the article teaches you about Emotional development and how you can apply that to your life and work.

4. Developmental Problems – As with most theories and areas of personal development, there is a normal way a person will develop. Identify examples of a person having other than normal Emotional development and factors that could contribute to that from the perspectives of both nature and nurture.

5. Application to Life and Work – Reflect on application of personal Emotional development to your own life and work right now.
   a. How does the description of normal Emotional development fit your own life now?
   b. How does the description of normal Emotional development fit with the work that you do or that you plan to do?
   c. How does this the description of normal Emotional development fit with the significant other people in your life – family, best friends, co-workers, life partners, etc?

Practice Test Items

1. Describe Emotional development from birth to age six.
    a. Normal development
    b. Some dysfunctional development issues that can occur during this time of life.

2. Describe Emotional development from age six to age 11.
    a. Normal development
    b. Some dysfunctional development issues that can occur during this time of life.

3. Describe Emotional development from age 12 to age 18.
    a. Normal development
    b. Some dysfunctional development issues that can occur during this time of life.

4. Describe Emotional development during Early and Middle Adulthood.
    a. Normal development
    b. Some dysfunctional development issues that can occur during this time of life.

5. Describe Emotional development during Late Adulthood.
    a. Normal development
    b. Some dysfunctional development issues that can occur during this time of life.

Additional Resources

Textbooks

Santrock, J. (2013). *Life-span development*. (15th ed.). Boston: McGraw-Hill Publishers. NOTE: McGraw-Hill also offers an online resource to accompany this text- *Connect*.

Sigelman, C.K. & Rider, E.A. (2014). *Life-span human development* (8th ed.). Belmont, CA: Wadsworth Cengage Learning.

Woolfolk, A. & Perry, N.E. (2015). *Child and Adolescent Development* (2nd ed.). Upper Saddle River, NJ: Pearson.

Web Links

http://www.education.com/reference/article/emotional-development/

http://www.focusonthefamily.com/parenting/your-childs-emotions/emotional-development/your-childs-emotions-overview

http://www.emotionaldevelopment.org/

https://www.youtube.com/watch?v=IDs6r9_Fzxw

https://www.youtube.com/watch?v=pignLj_bPsE

Tips for Instructors

While students may easily learn rote facts about the theories, they can better learn application of the theories to life-span development through opportunities for application. Examples are provided in this chapter and with each chapter on the theories for exam items and assignments that can promote integration of theory to life.

Tips for Students

These theories of life-span development provide core understanding of why we live the way we live. To borrow a concept from health care, understanding involves identification of the evidence. As you apply a theory to your life or the life of someone else, think about what is the evidence that you or the other person is representing that facet of that theory.

Moral

Background

Moral Development involves growth in a person's understanding and actions with rules and expectations on what should be done as people interact with each other.

Exercises

1. Journaling – Begin a journal as you studies the theories and areas of lifespan development and write reflections about yourself for each studied. For Moral development, describe what you remember about yourself about this area of development.

2. Observation - Use your journal to take notes from observation of several people whom you know well, such as family, friends, or co-workers. As with yourself, note how the person demonstrates his or her Moral development.

3. Research – Find a scholarly article on Cognitive development and summarize that to share with your class. Focus on what the article teaches you about Moral development and how you can apply that to your life and work.

4. Developmental Problems – As with most theories and areas of personal development, there is a normal way a person will develop. Identify examples of a person having other than normal Moral development and factors that could contribute to that from the perspectives of both nature and nurture.

5. Application to Life and Work – Reflect on application of personal Moral development to your own life and work right now.
   a. How does the description of normal Moral development fit your own life now?
   b. How does the description of normal Moral development fit with the work that you do or that you plan to do?
   c. How does this the description of normal Moral development fit with the significant other people in your life – family, best friends, co-workers, life partners, etc?

Practice Test Items

1. Describe Moral development from birth to age six.
    a. Normal development
    b. Some dysfunctional development issues that can occur during this time of life.

2. Describe Moral development from age six to age 11.
    a. Normal development
    b. Some dysfunctional development issues that can occur during this time of life.

3. Describe Moral development from age 12 to age 18.
    a. Normal development
    b. Some dysfunctional development issues that can occur during this time of life.

4. Describe Moral development during Early and Middle Adulthood.
    a. Normal development
    b. Some dysfunctional development issues that can occur during this time of life.

5. Describe Moral development during Late Adulthood.
    a. Normal development
    b. Some dysfunctional development issues that can occur during this time of life.

Additional Resources

Textbooks

Santrock, J. (2013). *Life-span development.* (15th ed.). Boston: McGraw-Hill Publishers. NOTE: McGraw-Hill also offers an online resource to accompany this text- *Connect.*

Sigelman, C.K. & Rider, E.A. (2014). *Life-span human development* (8th ed.). Belmont, CA: Wadsworth Cengage Learning.

Woolfolk, A. & Perry, N.E. (2015). *Child and Adolescent Development* (2nd ed.). Upper Saddle River, NJ: Pearson.

Web Links

https://www.mentalhelp.net/articles/early-childhood-moral-development/

http://www.earlychildhoodnews.com/earlychildhood/article_view.aspx?ArticleID=118

http://parenthood.library.wisc.edu/Berkowitz/Berkowitz.html

http://www.lenearnettjensen.com/moral-development-articles/

https://docs.gatesfoundation.org/documents/successfuldevelopment.pdf

Tips for Instructors

While students may easily learn rote facts about the theories, they can better learn application of the theories to life-span development through opportunities for application. Examples are provided in this chapter and with each chapter on the theories for exam items and assignments that can promote integration of theory to life.

Tips for Students

These theories of life-span development provide core understanding of why we live the way we live. To borrow a concept from health care, understanding involves identification of the evidence. As you apply a theory to your life or the life of someone else, think about what is the evidence that you or the other person is representing that facet of that theory.

Physical

Background

Physical Development involves growth and functioning of our bodies. This development is reflected through maintaining optimal health by getting enough sleep, eating healthy, exercising, and avoiding unhealthy habits. It can also be reflected through practice of negative health habits such as negligence of one's body or practice of habits that are harmful to one's physical health.

Exercises

1. Journaling – Begin a journal as you studies the theories and areas of lifespan development and write reflections about yourself for each studied. For Physical development, describe what you remember about yourself about this area of development..

2. Observation - Use your journal to take notes from observation of several people whom you know well, such as family, friends, or co-workers. As with yourself, note how the person demonstrates his or her Physical development.

3. Research – Find a scholarly article on Physical development and summarize that to share with your class. Focus on what the article teaches you about Physical development and how you can apply that to your life and work.

4. Developmental Problems – As with most theories and areas of personal development, there is a normal way a person will develop. Identify examples of a person having other than normal Physical development and factors that could contribute to that from the perspectives of both nature and nurture.

5. Application to Life and Work – Reflect on application of personal Physical development to your own life and work right now.
   a. How does the description of normal Physical development fit your own life now?
   b. How does the description of normal Physical development fit with the work that you do or that you plan to do?
   c. How does this the description of normal Physical development

fit with the significant other people in your life – family, best friends, co-workers, life partners, etc?

Practice Test Items

1. Describe Physical development from birth to age six.
    a. Normal development
    b. Some dysfunctional development issues that can occur during this time of life.

2. Describe Physical development from age six to age 11.
    a. Normal development
    b. Some dysfunctional development issues that can occur during this time of life.

3. Describe Physical development from age 12 to age 18.
    a. Normal development
    b. Some dysfunctional development issues that can occur during this time of life.

4. Describe Physical development during Early and Middle Adulthood.
    a. Normal development
    b. Some dysfunctional development issues that can occur during this time of life.

5. Describe Physical development during Late Adulthood.
    a. Normal development
    b. Some dysfunctional development issues that can occur during this time of life.

Additional Resources

Textbooks

Santrock, J. (2013). *Life-span development.* (15th ed.). Boston: McGraw-Hill Publishers. NOTE: McGraw-Hill also offers an online resource to accompany this text- *Connect.*

Sigelman, C.K. & Rider, E.A. (2014). *Life-span human development* (8th ed.). Belmont, CA: Wadsworth Cengage Learning.

Woolfolk, A. & Perry, N.E. (2015). *Child and Adolescent Development* (2nd ed.). Upper Saddle River, NJ: Pearson.

Web Links

http://www.kidspot.com.au/parenting/toddler/toddler-development/1-2-years-physical-development-1

http://www.gracepointwellness.org/462-child-development-parenting-early-3-7/article/12755-early-childhood-physical-development-gross-and-fine-motor-development

http://www.aboutkidshealth.ca/En/HealthAZ/DevelopmentalStages/SchoolAgeChildren/Pages/Physical-Development.aspx

http://raisingchildren.net.au/articles/physical_changes_teenagers.html

https://www.boundless.com/psychology/textbooks/boundless-psychology-textbook/human-development-14/early-and-middle-adulthood-74/physical-development-in-adulthood-287-12822/

Tips for Instructors

While students may easily learn rote facts about the theories, they can better learn application of the theories to life-span development through opportunities for application. Examples are provided in this chapter and with each chapter on the theories for exam items and assignments that can promote integration of theory to life.

Tips for Students

These theories of life-span development provide core understanding of why we live the way we live. To borrow a concept from health care, understanding involves identification of the evidence. As you apply a theory to your life or the life of someone else, think about what is the evidence that you or the other person is representing that facet of that theory.

Social

Background

Social Development involves growth and functioning of our relationships and interactions with other people. This development is evidenced in the quality and extent of supportive social networks, personal contributions to society, and treatment of cultural diversity.

Exercises

1. Journaling – Begin a journal as you studies the theories and areas of lifespan development and write reflections about yourself for each studied. For Social development, describe what you remember about yourself about this area of development.

2. Observation - Use your journal to take notes from observation of several people whom you know well, such as family, friends, or co-workers. As with yourself, note how the person demonstrates his or her Social development.

3. Research – Find a scholarly article on Cognitive development and summarize that to share with your class. Focus on what the article teaches you about Social development and how you can apply that to your life and work.

4. Developmental Problems – As with most theories and areas of personal development, there is a normal way a person will develop. Identify examples of a person having other than normal Social development and factors that could contribute to that from the perspectives of both nature and nurture.

5. Application to Life and Work – Reflect on application of personal Social development to your own life and work right now.
   a. How does the description of normal Social development fit your own life now?
   b. How does the description of normal Social development fit with the work that you do or that you plan to do?
   c. How does this the description of normal Social development fit with the significant other people in your life – family, best friends, co-workers, life partners, etc?

Practice Test Items

1. Describe Social development from birth to age six.
   a. Normal development
   b. Some dysfunctional development issues that can occur during this time of life.

2. Describe Social development from age six to age 11.
   a. Normal development
   b. Some dysfunctional development issues that can occur during this time of life.

3. Describe Social development from age 12 to age 18.
   a. Normal development
   b. Some dysfunctional development issues that can occur during this time of life.

4. Describe Social development during Early and Middle Adulthood.
   a. Normal development
   b. Some dysfunctional development issues that can occur during this time of life.
   c. Describe Social development during Late Adulthood.
   d. Normal development
   e. Some dysfunctional development issues that can occur during this time of life.

Additional Resources

Textbooks

Santrock, J. (2013). *Life-span development.* (15th ed.). Boston: McGraw-Hill Publishers. NOTE: McGraw-Hill also offers an online resource to accompany this text- *Connect.*

Sigelman, C.K. & Rider, E.A. (2014). *Life-span human development* (8th ed.). Belmont, CA: Wadsworth Cengage Learning.

Woolfolk, A. & Perry, N.E. (2015). *Child and Adolescent Development* (2nd ed.). Upper Saddle River, NJ: Pearson.

Web Links

http://www.scilearn.com/blog/how-to-support-social-development-in-young-children

https://www.healthychildren.org/English/ages-stages/preschool/Pages/Social-Development-in-Preschoolers.aspx

http://my.clevelandclinic.org/childrens-hospital/health-info/ages-stages/adolescence/hic-Social-Development-During-the-Teen-Years

http://www.aboutkidshealth.ca/En/HealthAZ/DevelopmentalStages/SchoolAgeChildren/Pages/Social-and-Emotional-Development.aspx

http://study.com/academy/lesson/social-development-of-adults-self-concept.html

Tips for Instructors

While students may easily learn rote facts about the theories, they can better learn application of the theories to life-span development through opportunities for application. Examples are provided in this chapter and with each chapter on the theories for exam items and assignments that can promote integration of theory to life.

Tips for Students

These theories of life-span development provide core understanding of why we live the way we live. To borrow a concept from health care, understanding involves identification of the evidence. As you apply a theory to your life or the life of someone else, think about what is the evidence that you or the other person is representing that facet of that theory.

Cultural

Background

Cultural Development involves growth and functioning within "shared values, beliefs, expectations, worldview, symbols, and appropriate learned behaviors of a group that provide its members with norms, plans, traditions, and rules for social living." (Gladding, 2011, p. 44)

Exercises

1. Journaling – Begin a journal as you studies the theories and areas of lifespan development and write reflections about yourself for each studied. For Cultural development, describe what you remember about yourself about this area of development.

2. Observation - Use your journal to take notes from observation of several people whom you know well, such as family, friends, or co-workers. As with yourself, note how the person demonstrates his or her Cultural development.

3. Research – Find a scholarly article on Cultural development and summarize that to share with your class. Focus on what the article teaches you about Cognitive development and how you can apply that to your life and work.

4. Developmental Problems – As with most theories and areas of personal development, there is a normal way a person will develop. Identify examples of a person having other than normal Cultural development and factors that could contribute to that from the perspectives of both nature and nurture.

5. Application to Life and Work – Reflect on application of personal Cultural development to your own life and work right now.
   a. How does the description of normal Cultural development fit your own life now?
   b. How does the description of normal Cultural development fit with the work that you do or that you plan to do?
   c. How does this the description of normal Cultural development fit with the significant other people in your life – family, best friends, co-workers, life partners, etc?

Practice Test Items

1. Describe Cultural development from birth to age six.
   a. Normal development
   b. Some dysfunctional development issues that can occur during this time of life.

2. Describe Cultural development from age six to age 11.
   a. Normal development
   b. Some dysfunctional development issues that can occur during this time of life.

3. Describe Cultural development from age 12 to age 18.
   a. Normal development
   b. Some dysfunctional development issues that can occur during this time of life.

4. Describe Cultural development during Early and Middle Adulthood.
   a. Normal development
   b. Some dysfunctional development issues that can occur during this time of life.

1. Describe Cultural development during Late Adulthood.
   a. Normal development
   b. Some dysfunctional development issues that can occur during this time of life.

Additional Resources

Textbooks

Santrock, J. (2013). *Life-span development.* (15th ed.). Boston: McGraw-Hill Publishers. NOTE: McGraw-Hill also offers an online resource to accompany this text- *Connect.*

Sigelman, C.K. & Rider, E.A. (2014). *Life-span human development* (8th ed.). Belmont, CA: Wadsworth Cengage Learning.

Woolfolk, A. & Perry, N.E. (2015). *Child and Adolescent Development* (2nd ed.). Upper Saddle River, NJ: Pearson.

Web Links

http://www.cultureindevelopment.nl/

http://www.kidsmatter.edu.au/early-childhood/about-social-development/about-welcoming-cultural-diversity/why-culture-matters

http://oureverydaylife.com/cultural-differences-development-children-18936.html

http://www.uua.org/sites/live-new.uua.org/files/documents/derman-sparkslouise/1206_233_identity_stages.pdf

https://www.boundless.com/psychology/textbooks/boundless-psychology-textbook/human-development-14/aging-late-adulthood-412/how-culture-and-society-impact-the-elderly-293-12828/

Tips for Instructors

While students may easily learn rote facts about the theories, they can better learn application of the theories to life-span development through opportunities for application. Examples are provided in this chapter and with each chapter on the theories for exam items and assignments that can promote integration of theory to life.

Tips for Students

These theories of life-span development provide core understanding of why we live the way we live. To borrow a concept from health care, understanding involves identification of the evidence. As you apply a theory to your life or the life of someone else, think about what is the evidence that you or the other person is representing that facet of that theory.

CHAPTER 4

Application to Lifespan Stages

Background

Course textbooks discuss development of individuals in the above areas for each Lifespan stage. This workbook will facilitate student conceptualization of total person development in each of the following lifespan stages. The key focus of this workbook is exploration of theory application and the five areas of personal development for each of the following lifespan stages as covered in section IV. Each of these chapters begins with the description of that period of development as provided by Santrock (2015).

- Beginnings – Conception to Birth.
- Infancy – birth to 24 months.
- Early Childhood – 2 – 5 years.
- Middle to Late Childhood – 6 – 11 years.
- Adolescence – 12 – 20 years.
- Early Adulthood - 20s and 30s.
- Middle Adulthood – 40s and 50s.
- Late Adulthood – 60s and beyond
- Endings – Death

Exercises

1. Reflect back on your own life and describe the highlights that you remember of each stage to this point in your life, either from your own memory or from what someone has told you about that part of your life, such as a parent or grandparent.

2. Through research of literature or even current news publications, list what seem to be the key challenges in your country for each life-span stage.

3. Through research of literature or even current news publications, describe what could be your future challenges for the life-span stages you have yet to experience.

Note on Case Studies: A case study is provided in the chapter for each life-span stage that presents developmental considerations for an individual in that period of life-span development. Some of these studies have been shared by students who took a course in Life-Span Development and some have been retrieved from different websites - therefore the format and sections of studies may differ across the stages, but will still give a good portrayal of comprehensive development at that stage of life.

Practice Test Items

Note: The Practice Test Items in this Section on life-span stages will integrate with your text and other resources from which you study for your course.

1. One of the developmental issues across the life-span is that of nature versus nurture. Nature is referred to a person's biological/genetic inheritance and nurture is referred to environmental experiences. Discuss the following:
   a. The extent to which of each of these have formed your own life development.
   b. Your thoughts on the degree to which each of these contribute to routine development of any person.
2. Discuss the notion that chronological age, biological age, psychological age, and social age of a person may not all be the same.
3. Discuss your understanding of the following characteristics of life-span development.
   a. Development is lifelong
   b. Development is multidimensional
   c. Development is multidirectional
   d. Development is contextual
   e. Development has capacity for change

Additional Resources

Textbooks

Santrock, J. (2015). *Life-span development.* (15th ed.). Boston: McGraw-Hill Publishers. NOTE: McGraw-Hill also offers an online resource to accompany this text- *Connect.*

Sigelman, C.K. & Rider, E.A. (2014). *Life-span human development* (8th ed.). Belmont, CA: Wadsworth Cengage Learning.

Woolfolk, A. & Perry, N.E. (2015). *Child and Adolescent Development* (2nd ed.). Upper Saddle River, NJ: Pearson.

Web Links

http://www.psych.purdue.edu/~willia55/120/5.DevMM.pdf

http://infed.org/mobi/life-span-development-and-lifelong-learning/

http://www.sulross.edu/sites/default/files/sites/default/files/users/docs/education/counseling-hgd_7.pdf

http://www.noteaccess.com/APPROACHES/ArtEd/ChildDev/BtD.htm

http://www.lifeopedia.com/different-needs-for-the-different-stages-of-our-lives/

Tips for Instructors

While students may easily learn rote facts about the theories, they can better learn application of the theories to life-span development through opportunities for application. Examples are provided in this chapter and with each chapter on the theories for exam items and assignments that can promote integration of theory to life.

Tips for Students

These theories of life-span development provide core understanding of why we live the way we live. To borrow a concept from health care, understanding involves identification of the evidence. As you apply a theory to your life or the life of someone else, think about what is the evidence that you or the other person is representing that facet of that theory.

Beginnings

Background

This is the first period of development in life. It is "the time from conception to birth. It involves tremendous growth – from a single cell to an organism complete with brain and behavioral capabilities – and takes place in approximately a 9-month period." (Santrock, 2015, p. 13).

Exercises

1. Journaling – Begin a journal as you study the theories of lifespan development and write reflections about yourself for each theory and stage studied. For the Beginnings stage, describe what you remember about yourself for this stage – you may have to ask parents or other care-givers about that time in your life, but do note any memories that you do have.

2. Observation - Use your journal to take notes from observation of a few people who are currently in the Beginnings stage. As with yourself, note how the person demonstrates what you are learning about that stage.

3. Research – Find a scholarly article on the Beginnings stage of life and summarize that to share with your class. Focus on what the article teaches you about Beginnings and how you can apply that to your life and work.

4. Developmental Problems – Discuss developmental problems that you have learned about with the Beginnings stage of life.
   a. Through some research about this.
   b. Through your own knowledge and observations about current events and people.

5. Application to Life and Work – Reflect on application of knowledge about the Beginnings stage; to your own life and work right now.
   a. How does knowledge of this stage fit your own life now?
   b. How does knowledge of this stage fit with the work that you do or that you plan to do?
   c. How does knowledge of this stage fit with the significant other people in your life – family, best friends, co-workers, life partners, etc?

Case Study

This website provides an in-depth interactive study on a couple, Molly and Rick who are excitedly preparing for the birth of their new baby. The case study provides much information on considerations while a baby is still in the Beginnings stage of development. http://www.genomicseducation.ca/prenatal_case/book.html

Practice Test Items

1. What are factors on the part of both the mother and the father that can influence prenatal development of child?

2. Describe the key events in development in the three trimesters of prenatal development.

3. Describe several environmental teratogens that can impact prenatal development.

4. Describe the three stages of the birth process.

5. Describe three assessment tools that are used with newborns.

Additional Resources

Textbooks

Santrock, J. (2015). *Life-span development.* (15th ed.). Boston: McGraw-Hill Publishers. NOTE: McGraw-Hill also offers an online resource to accompany this text- *Connect.*

Sigelman, C.K. & Rider, E.A. (2014). *Life-span human development* (8th ed.). Belmont, CA: Wadsworth Cengage Learning.

Woolfolk, A. & Perry, N.E. (2015). *Child and Adolescent Development* (2nd ed.). Upper Saddle River, NJ: Pearson.

Web Links

https://www.youtube.com/watch?v=AvB0q3mg4sQ

https://my.clevelandclinic.org/health/diseases_conditions/hic_Am_I_Pregnant/hic-fetal-development-stages-of-growth

http://www.ncbi.nlm.nih.gov/pmc/articles/PMC2529423/

http://www.aboutkidshealth.ca/en/resourcecentres/pregnancybabies/Pregnancy/FetalDevelopment/Pages/default.aspx

https://www.boundless.com/psychology/textbooks/boundless-psychology-textbook/human-development-14/prenatal-development-71/environmental-impacts-on-prenatal-development-274-12809/

Tips for Instructors

While students may easily learn rote facts about the theories, they can better learn application of the theories to life-span development through opportunities for application. Examples are provided in this chapter and with each chapter on the theories for exam items and assignments that can promote integration of theory to life.

Tips for Students

These theories of life-span development provide core understanding of why we live the way we live. To borrow a concept from health care, understanding involves identification of the evidence. As you apply a theory to your life or the life of someone else, think about what is the evidence that you or the other person is representing that facet of that theory.

Infancy

Background

This is "the developmental period from birth to 18 or 24 months. Infancy is a time of extreme dependence upon adults. During this period, many psychological activities – language, symbolic thought, sensorimotor coordination, and social learning, for example – are just beginning." (Santrock, 2015, p. 13).

Exercises

1. Journaling – Begin a journal as you study the theories of lifespan development and write reflections about yourself for each theory and stage studied. For the Infancy stage, describe what you remember about yourself for this stage – you may have to ask parents or other care-givers about that time in your life, but do note any memories that you do have.

2. Observation - Use your journal to take notes from observation of a few people who are currently in the Infancy stage. As with yourself, note how the person demonstrates what you are learning about that stage.

3. Research – Find a scholarly article on the Beginnings stage of life and summarize that to share with your class. Focus on what the article teaches you about Infancy and how you can apply that to your life and work.

4. Developmental Problems – Discuss developmental problems that you have learned about with the Infancy stage of life.
    a. Through some research about this.
    b. Through your own knowledge and observations about current events and people.

5. Application to Life and Work – Reflect on application of knowledge about the Infancy stage; to your own life and work right now.
    a. How does knowledge of this stage fit your own life now?
    b. How does knowledge of this stage fit with the work that you do or that you plan to do?
    c. How does knowledge of this stage fit with the significant other people in your life – family, best friends, co-workers, life partners, etc?

Case Study with Integration of Piaget's Theory

This is a case study of an individual in the infancy life-span stage. This study is focused on a 10 month old, Caucasian, male that we will identify as BG. BG lives with his mother, father and two older siblings, his brother is four years old and sister is three years old. He attends a full time daycare facility during the school year from 7:30am-5:00pm Monday thru Friday. At his daycare he is in the care of two adult females, he spends his day with 4-5 other babies under the age of 12 months. During the summer months of June thru August he stays at home with all of his family members.

Application of Piaget Theory

BG fits into Piaget's sensorimotor stage. He falls within the age range of birth to 2 years old. In this stage of his theory, infants construct an understanding of the world by coordinating sensory experiences with physical, motoric actions. BG uses his senses, physical abilities and body movement to learn about the world around him.

Cognitive Development

Piaget's sensorimotor stage is broken down into six sub stages progressing in order. The first one consists of simple reflexes. This occurs in the first month after birth. In this sub stage, sensation and action are coordinated through reflexive behaviors (Santrock 2015). The second sub stage, first habits and primary circular reactions, develops between the ages of 1 and 4 months. Here, infants coordinate sensation and two types of schemes, habits and primary circular reactions (Santrock 2015). The third sub stages is secondary circular reactions, this takes place between 4-8 months of age. During this stage infants become more object oriented (Santrock 2015). The four sub stage, coordination of secondary circular reactions, is from 8-12 months old, and uses the coordination of sight and touch. The fifth sub stage is, tertiary circular reactions such as novelty and curiosity. During this time infants become intrigued by the many things that they can do with objects (Santrock 2015). The final sub stage is, internalization of schemes. This takes place when infants use their ability to use primitive symbols and form enduring mental representations (Santrock 2015). BG's current cognitive development level would take place in the tertiary circular reactions, novelty, and curiosity stage. He enjoys pushing things to watch them move, and hitting two objects together to hear the sound they can create. He also likes to throw things and then look at them when they land, and wonder how they got there.

Physical Development

BG is currently in very good health, and is up to date on all of his shots. He usually drinks an average of 6-8 ounces of breast milk 4-5 times a day. He also consumes two meals a day consisting of fruits, vegetables and meats in the form of finger food. He requires two 2-3 hour naps daily, as well as, 9 hours of sleep at night. He gets most of his current exercise from crawling and pulling himself up on furniture.

Emotional Development

BG would be classified as a happy, laidback baby. He loves to laugh and smile at friends and family members. He also loves to sit back and observe others. He watches his parents and siblings play together and watches them as they eat their food. He is content sitting on someone's lap, just hanging out. When he is upset, he makes sure that everyone knows it. First, he will make a face at you, sticking his lower lip out. Then, he will let out a loud yell and start crying. Sometimes he will begin flailing his arms to get more attention and let people around him know what he wants. When he is happy he will laugh and cuddle into you giving you kisses.

Social Development

BG loves to talk in gibber. He really likes it when you talk to him, even if you aren't saying real words but are gibbering back. He also uses a lot of non-verbal's, such as shaking his head no, and swing his arms, and crawling at you with his mouth open to let you know that he wants your food. He loves to lay on his brother and "get him" or play with him by cuddling and giggling.

Moral Development

BG's current view of and practice of morality is that of the Heteronomous morality. He stops doing things he shouldn't do because his parents or older siblings tell him that he shouldn't do them. Some of these include trying to play with the DVD player, getting into the dog kennel and dog food, and biting because he gets excited. When he is told to no-no, he will shake his head no. Sometimes he will stop what he is doing and move on to other things or cry because he really wants to do what you won't let him. Other times he will shake his head no and continue doing it.

Conclusion

In conclusion BG has shown progression in many of the sub stages laid out by Piaget's Theory for the sensorimotor stage. He started out with sucking and grasping then moved on to sucking his thumb along with toes and other parts of his body. Then he started using his hand-eye coordination to switch toys between his hands, get object to move closer to him, as well as get food to his mouth. Although he is currently only 10 months old, he falls into sub category 5 which consists of being intrigued with the many properties of an object. According to Piaget this doesn't happen till around 12-18 months of age. On the contrary, BG did not start cooing or crying to get a person to stay in the room or near him till he was about 9 ½ months old. This would be a little behind the developmental norm.

Practice Test Items

1. Describe Kangaroo Care.
2. Describe the nutrition needs of infants and the benefits as well as challenges of breast feeding.
3. Describe affordances.
4. Describe four reflexes that infants have.
5. Describe the process of language development with infants.

Additional Resources

Textbooks

Santrock, J. (2015). *Life-span development.* (15th ed.). Boston: McGraw-Hill Publishers. NOTE: McGraw-Hill also offers an online resource to accompany this text- *Connect.*

Sigelman, C.K. & Rider, E.A. (2014). *Life-span human development* (8th ed.). Belmont, CA: Wadsworth Cengage Learning.

Woolfolk, A. & Perry, N.E. (2015). *Child and Adolescent Development* (2nd ed.). Upper Saddle River, NJ: Pearson.

Web Links

http://parenting.adoption.com/parents/adoption-and-the-stages-of-development.html

http://www.mayoclinic.org/healthy-living/infant-and-toddler-health/in-depth/infant-development/art-20048012

http://www.babycenter.com/milestone-charts-birth-to-age-3

http://www.livescience.com/20802-newborn-baby-skills.html

http://www.webmd.com/parenting/baby/infant-development-9/

Tips for Instructors

While students may easily learn rote facts about the theories, they can better learn application of the theories to life-span development through opportunities for application. Examples are provided in this chapter and with each chapter on the theories for exam items and assignments that can promote integration of theory to life.

Tips for Students

These theories of life-span development provide core understanding of why we live the way we live. To borrow a concept from health care, understanding involves identification of the evidence. As you apply a theory to your life or the life of someone else, think about what is the evidence that you or the other person is representing that facet of that theory.

Early Childhood

Background

This is "the developmental period from 3 through 5 years of age. This period is sometimes called the preschool years. During this time, young children learn to become more self-sufficient and to care for themselves, develop school readiness skills (following instructions, identifying letters), and spend many hours playing with peers. First grade typically marks the end of early childhood. (Santrock, 2015, p. 13)

Exercises

1. Journaling – Begin a journal as you study the theories of lifespan development and write reflections about yourself for each theory and stage studied. For the Early Childhood stage, describe what you remember about yourself for this stage – you may have to ask parents or other care-givers about that time in your life, but do note any memories that you do have.

2. Observation - Use your journal to take notes from observation of a few people who are currently in the Early Childhood stage. As with yourself, note how the person demonstrates what you are learning about that stage.

3. Research – Find a scholarly article on the Early Childhood stage of life and summarize that to share with your class. Focus on what the article teaches you about Early Childhood and how you can apply that to your life and work.

4. Developmental Problems – Discuss developmental problems that you have learned about with the Early Childhood stage of life.
    a. Through some research about this.
    b. Through your own knowledge and observations about current events and people.

5. Application to Life and Work – Reflect on application of knowledge about the Early Childhood stage; to your own life and work right now.
    a. How does knowledge of this stage fit your own life now?
    b. How does knowledge of this stage fit with the work that you do or that you plan to do?

c. How does knowledge of this stage fit with the significant other people in your life – family, best friends, co-workers, life partners, etc?

Case Study with Integration of Erikson's Theory

This is a case study of an individual in the early childhood life-span stage. The person I will be doing this case study on is a four year old white female. She lives with her mother, father, and little brother in Cumming, GA. This child does not go to preschool and she stays at home with his mother all day. She will be starting pre-K in the fall. I will be describing how Erikson's theory applies to WH and how she is developing cognitively, physically, emotionally, socially, and morally.

Application of Erickson's Theory

In Erikson's theory, people go through eight stages of development throughout their lifetime. Erikson believes that at each stage in our life, we have a developmental crisis that must be resolved (Santrock, 2015). For example, in early childhood, as the child encounters a widening social world, the child is confronted with initiative vs. guilt (Santrock, 2015). In this developmental stage, the preschool aged child will face new challenges that may require responsible behavior. Instead, the child may feel guilt of being irresponsible.

Although WH has not entered preschool yet, she is constantly surrounded by friends and family. Through these interactions, her social world has been widened. WH has started to get a mind of her own and beginning to develop self-understanding. She has started using her own motor, cognitive, and language skills to make things happen. She has also started questioning why she has different body parts than her little brother. I believe that through these questions, WH will begin to develop more self-understanding.

Cognitive Development

As a child develops cognitively, the attention span also improves significantly (Santrock, 2015). I have witnessed WH sit and watch television or color in a coloring book for a half hour or more. Although WH is not yet in preschool, she has learned to read small words and also has a significant vocabulary for a four year old. Her mother constantly works with her on her language development and literacy skills. I believe that when she begins preschool, she will be more cognitively developed than some of the other children.

Physical Development

The average child grows 2 ½ inches and gained about 5 to 7 pounds a year (Santrock, 2015). Also, a child's brain will have the most rapid growth in the early childhood years, mainly in the frontal lobes (Santrock, 2015). WH weighs 38 pounds and is 3 feet, 2 inches tall. She is not a picky eater and her mother makes sure she has a healthy diet of vegetables and proteins. She sleeps on average of eight hours a night. WH is very healthy physically.

Emotional Development

Children will experience many emotions throughout the day. As a child becomes emotionally developed, he or she will begin to make sense of other people's emotions as well as begin to control their own (Santrock, 2015). WH is full of emotions. She is a very strong willed child and you always know exactly how she is feeling. Most of the time she is very happy but she has her emotional moments. She doesn't hold her emotions in and lets her mother and father know when she does not want to do something. Her favorite word right now is "no."

Social Development

WH mainly interacts with her parents, grandparents, brother, and cousins. Because she has not started preschool yet, she has not had the chance to interact with many other children her age. She interacts with her family in a positive way most of the time. She has her moments when she throws tantrums if she does not get her way, but most of the time, she is a very happy child.

Moral Development

According to Kohlberg's theory on moral development, WH is in the heteronomous morality stage (Santrock, 2015). She worries about being punished if she disobeys her parents. She bases her decisions of behavior based on how her parents will react.

WH has moved into the Individualism, instrumental purpose, and exchange stage. She pursues her own interests but lets her little brother or old cousin do the same. I have also witnessed her being sweet to her older cousin CM and then get upset when he is mean to her.

Conclusion

WH seems to be developing on an above average level. Because she was first born and had her constant attention of her parents for the first couple of years of her life, she has learned more than most children. As when she starts preschool, she should not have any problems learning and interacting with the other children.

Practice Test Items

1. Describe different types of temperament with young children.

2. Describe Bowlby's Attachment Theory.

3. Describe four different formats for early childhood education.

4. Describe Parenting Styles.

5. Describe four different types of maltreatment to watch for with younger children.

Additional Resources

Textbooks

Santrock, J. (2015). *Life-span development*. (15th ed.). Boston: McGraw-Hill Publishers. NOTE: McGraw-Hill also offers an online resource to accompany this text- *Connect.*

Sigelman, C.K. & Rider, E.A. (2014). *Life-span human development* (8th ed.). Belmont, CA: Wadsworth Cengage Learning.

Woolfolk, A. & Perry, N.E. (2015). *Child and Adolescent Development* (2nd ed.). Upper Saddle River, NJ: Pearson.

Web Links

http://www.npr.org/sections/ed/2014/08/28/343735856/kids-and-screen-time-what-does-the-research-say

http://centerforparentingeducation.org/library-of-articles/discipline-topics/effective-parenting-style-discipline-works/

https://www.youtube.com/watch?v=z6yp5tnLmys

http://www.simplypsychology.org/bowlby.html

http://www.developmentalscreening.org/screening_tools/denverii.htm

Tips for Instructors

While students may easily learn rote facts about the theories, they can better learn application of the theories to life-span development through opportunities for application. Examples are provided in this chapter and with each chapter on the theories for exam items and assignments that can promote integration of theory to life.

Tips for Students

These theories of life-span development provide core understanding of why we live the way we live. To borrow a concept from health care, understanding involves identification of the evidence. As you apply a theory to your life or the life of someone else, think about what is the evidence that you or the other person is representing that facet of that theory.

Middle to Late Childhood

Background

This is "the developmental period from about 6 to 10 or 11 years of age, approximately corresponding to the elementary school years. During this period, children master the fundamental skills of reading, writing, and arithmetic, and they are formally exposed to the larger world and its culture. Achievement becomes a more central theme of the child's world, and self-control increases." (Santrock, 2015, p. 14).

Exercises

1. Journaling – Begin a journal as you study the theories of lifespan development and write reflections about yourself for each theory and stage studied. For the Middle to Late Childhood stage, describe what you remember about yourself for this stage – you may have to ask parents or other care-givers about that time in your life, but do note any memories that you do have.

2. Observation - Use your journal to take notes from observation of a few people who are currently in the Middle to Late Childhood stage. As with yourself, note how the person demonstrates what you are learning about that stage.

3. Research – Find a scholarly article on the Middle to Late Childhood stage of life and summarize that to share with your class. Focus on what the article teaches you about Middle to Late Childhood and how you can apply that to your life and work.

4. Developmental Problems – Discuss developmental problems that you have learned about with the Middle to Late Childhood stage of life.
    a. Through some research about this.
    b. Through your own knowledge and observations about current events and people.

5. Application to Life and Work – Reflect on application of knowledge about the Middle to Late Childhood stage; to your own life and work right now.
    a. How does knowledge of this stage fit your own life now?
    b. How does knowledge of this stage fit with the work that you do or that you plan to do?

c. How does knowledge of this stage fit with the significant other people in your life – family, best friends, co-workers, life partners, etc?

Case Study with Integration of Bandura's Theory

This is a case study on an individual in the Middle Childhood development stage. Being only referred to as S.L. this individual is a 5 year old Caucasian female. S.L. lives with her Mother, Father, and younger Sister. Having two parents who work full time has allowed S.L. the opportunity to attend Pre-K programs until she is able to start school in August of this year.

Application of Albert Bandura's Social Cognitive Theory

Concentrating on ability of being able to do something and mastering that skill is important to realize during this case study. The ability to say "I can" is a development is cognitive thought that most children should be able to grasp. According to Santrock(2015), page 320, "Students with high self efficacy endorse such statements as "I know that I will be able to learn the material in this class" and "I expect to be able to do well at this activity". On a recent observation, S.L. was taken to an indoor play center and told to go play. She played for a moment but quickly shut down when she could not figure out how to do one of the activities. After a while of sitting, she went back and tried the activity one more time and this time was able to accomplish the goal of finishing the activity. The look on her face was as if she had just conquered the world. It was amazing to see how trying one more time, she was able to accomplish the goal and in turn, feel better about herself. She was so very proud. After this accomplishment, she went on to a few other activities and showed great confidence when confronting things that challenged her.

Cognitive Development

Judging cognitive development of S.L. has proven to be confusing. She has minimal to normal verbal communication skills and is generally introverted. She is content being alone and seemed to get very uneasy when faced with new situations or events surrounding her that were outside of her comfort zone. Hopefully going to school in the fall will allow her to open up and develop more cognitively as she is faced with new scenarios.

Physical Development

S.L. is in great health. She was born at term and has had very few complications in her short life. She eats a normal diet and exercises frequently by playing outdoors and doing a weekly dance class. She seems to be allowed minimal screen time which will hopefully help her with her cognitive development.

Emotional Development

S.L. seems to be struggling emotionally. She is very attached and not well adjusted when faced with new opportunities in life. I feel that she has not been able to develop properly due to over protective parenting and very little individualization.

Social Development

Once again, social development is a struggle. S.L. is not comfortable in social situations that tend to take her outside of her comfort zone. On the few occasions I have seen her open up, she does fabulous! My recommendations would be to allow her to have more opportunities to become more socially active and to really encourage her to reach out to new situations.

Moral Development

S.L. is doing great developing morally. She absolutely knows right from wrong and has the ability to make choices that are a great way to go. This has helped her confidence and her ability to branch out a little. Her parents are great with positive reinforcement and this acceptance has also helped her along.

Conclusion

After observing S.L., it is apparent that she needs to work on her social and cognitive development and in turn all else will fall into place. She is a bright, intelligent 5 year old who just needs a little encouragement sometimes. It seems as long as her parents continue to guide her along with her positive reinforcement she will be able to lead a healthy life.

Practice Test Items

1. Describe some strategies for increase of creative thinking
2. Describe some current considerations in bilingualism and second language earning
3. Describe developmental differences pertaining to gender.
4. Describe some moral developmental issues for this life-span stage.
5. Describe development of friendships and bullying issues

Additional Resources

Textbooks

Santrock, J. (2013). *Life-span development*. (15th ed.). Boston: McGraw-Hill Publishers. NOTE: McGraw-Hill also offers an online resource to accompany this text- *Connect.*

Sigelman, C.K. & Rider, E.A. (2014). *Life-span human development* (8th ed.). Belmont, CA: Wadsworth Cengage Learning.

Woolfolk, A. & Perry, N.E. (2015). *Child and Adolescent Development* (2nd ed.). Upper Saddle River, NJ: Pearson.

Web Links

https://www.healthychildren.org/English/ages-stages/gradeschool/Pages/How-to-Understand-Your-Childs-Temperament.aspx

https://www.youtube.com/watch?v=g8Kl8TFUURU

http://www.stopbullying.gov/index.html

http://www.blinn.edu/socialscience/ldthomas/2011%20Fall/Santrock%20PPT/santrockTLS_5_PPT_ch10.ppt

https://www.youtube.com/watch?v=tLiP4b-TPCA

Tips for Instructors

While students may easily learn rote facts about the theories, they can better learn application of the theories to life-span development through opportunities for application. Examples are provided in this chapter and with each chapter on the theories for exam items and assignments that can promote integration of theory to life.

Tips for Students

These theories of life-span development provide core understanding of why we live the way we live. To borrow a concept from health care, understanding involves identification of the evidence. As you apply a theory to your life or the life of someone else, think about what is the evidence that you or the other person is representing that facet of that theory.

Adolescence

Background

This is the developmental period of transition from childhood to early adulthood, entered at approximately 10 to 12 years of age and ending at 18 to 21 years of age. Adolescence begins with rapid physical changes—dramatic gains in height and weight, changes in body contour, and the development of sexual characteristics such as enlargement of the breasts, growth of pubic and facial hair, and deepening of the voice. At this point in development, the pursuit of independence and an identity are preeminent. Thought is more logical, abstract, and idealistic. More time is spent outside the family." (Santrock, 2015, p. 14).

Exercises

1. Journaling – Begin a journal as you study the theories of lifespan development and write reflections about yourself for each theory and stage studied. For the stage of Adolescence, describe what you remember about yourself for this stage – you may have to ask parents or other care-givers about that time in your life, but do note any memories that you do have.

2. Observation - Use your journal to take notes from observation of a few people who are currently in the stage of Adolescence. As with yourself, note how the person demonstrates what you are learning about that stage.

3. Research – Find a scholarly article on the stage of Adolescence in life and summarize that to share with your class. Focus on what the article teaches you about Adolescence and how you can apply that to your life and work.

4. Developmental Problems – Discuss developmental problems that you have learned about with the stage of Adolescence in life.
   a. Through some research about this.
   b. Through your own knowledge and observations about current events and people.

5. Application to Life and Work – Reflect on application of knowledge about the stage of Adolescence to your own life and work right now.

a. How does knowledge of this stage fit your own life now?
b. How does knowledge of this stage fit with the work that you do or that you plan to do?
c. How does knowledge of this stage fit with the significant other people in your life – family, best friends, co-workers, life partners, etc?

Case Study with Integration ov Vygotsky's Theory

This is a case study of ES in the adolescent life-span stage. ES is a 14 year old African American girl. ES lives at home with her mother, sister, and 2 children. ES is a freshmen in high school. ES is teenage mother. She has a 3 year old son and 1 year old daughter.

Application of Vygotsky Theory

ES fits with Vygotsky's theory because she has developed a way of thinking and understanding through social interaction. Santrock (2015) states that children's cognitive development depends on the tools provided by society and their minds are shaped by culture context in which they live. After children master mental tools, they become in charge of their own learning, by attending and remembering in an intentional and purposeful way.

Cognitive Development

Cognitively ES is above average. She is a sharp thinker. Compared to her 13 year old sister and peers, ES has excellent self-control. She has the ability to think critically and make decisions. This is indicator by her 4.0 GPA. She able to control her attention and stayed focused in spite of her circumstances.

Physical Development

Physically ES is healthy. Although she has gave birth twice, she has a petite athletic build. ES was the captain of her dance team before she became pregnant. ES is always well put together. Her hair and nails are always done. Her clothes are trendy. ES went through puberty early. She started her period at the age of 10. By the time she was 11, ES was fully developed. She looked much older than her peers.

Emotional Development

ES is a happy child. She is not seem to worry about anything. ES always offers compliments to other. Although ES's family helps her with the kids, ES seems to be well rounded. She knows how to keep everything balance. She is very neat and organized.

Social Development

ES gets along well with others. She is respectful toward her mother. ES and her sister are very close. They don't fight each other like some sisters do. ES does have friends. However because she has two kids to care for is not able to spend as much time having fun with her peers. ES does not attend many social events because of her kids. However her family does go out for family fun occasionally. ES enjoys bowling, shooting pool, video games, and miniature golf.

Moral Development

ES is a rule follower. She believes in the law and doing what is right. She is the kind of child that does not have to be told to do things twice. She is very responsible. ES tries her best to motivate others to follow rules and procedures both inside and outside of school. ES attends church with her family every Sunday. She does a good job of teaching her kids her kids the importance of following rules and procedures. Unlike her peers, ES does not tells untruths to her mother about anything.

Conclusion

Cognitively and emotionally ES is above average. However her physical development could be a concern later because she gave birth at such a young age. Socially her lack of attending social events, and hanging out with her friends could have a negative impact her later. In conclusion ES is developing appropriately.

Practice Test Items

1. What are the key aspects of puberty for males and for females?
2. What can be some benefit from parent-adolescent conflict?
3. Describe Egocentrism in adolescence.

4. Describe some key health concerns for adolescents.

5. Describe Identity Development with an adolescent.

Additional Resources

Textbooks

Santrock, J. (2015). *Life-span development*. (15th ed.). Boston: McGraw-Hill Publishers. NOTE: McGraw-Hill also offers an online resource to accompany this text- *Connect.*

Sigelman, C.K. & Rider, E.A. (2014). *Life-span human development* (8th ed.). Belmont, CA: Wadsworth Cengage Learning.

Woolfolk, A. & Perry, N.E. (2015). *Child and Adolescent Development* (2nd ed.). Upper Saddle River, NJ: Pearson.

Web Links

http://youth.gov/youth-topics/juvenile-justice/prevention-and-early-intervention

http://ahd1113.activehost.com/pdf/60549.pdf

https://www.apa.org/about/governance/president/suicidal-behavior-adolescents.pdf

https://www.healthychildren.org/English/ages-stages/teen/Pages/Stages-of-Adolescence.aspx

https://www.healthychildren.org/English/family-life/family-dynamics/communication-discipline/Pages/How-to-Communicate-with-a-Teenager.aspx

Tips for Instructors

While students may easily learn rote facts about the theories, they can better learn application of the theories to life-span development through opportunities for application. Examples are provided in this chapter and with each chapter on the theories for exam items and assignments that can promote integration of theory to life.

Tips for Students

These theories of life-span development provide core understanding of why we live the way we live. To borrow a concept from health care, understanding involves identification of the evidence. As you apply a theory to your life or the life of someone else, think about what is the evidence that you or the other person is representing that facet of that theory.

Early Adulthood

Background

This is "the developmental period that begins in the early twenties and lasts through the thirties. It is a time of establishing personal and economic independence, advancing in a career, and for many, selecting a mate, learning to live with that person in an intimate way, starting a family, and rearing children." (Santrock, 2015, p. 14)

Exercises

1. Journaling – Begin a journal as you study the theories of lifespan development and write reflections about yourself for each theory and stage studied. For the Early Adulthood stage, describe what you remember about yourself for this stage – you may have to ask parents or other care-givers about that time in your life, but do note any memories that you do have.

2. Observation - Use your journal to take notes from observation of a few people who are currently in the Early Adulthood stage. As with yourself, note how the person demonstrates what you are learning about that stage.

3. Research – Find a scholarly article on the Early Adulthood stage of life and summarize that to share with your class. Focus on what the article teaches you about Early Adulthood and how you can apply that to your life and work.

4. Developmental Problems – Discuss developmental problems that you have learned about with the Early Adulthood stage of life.
    a. Through some research about this.
    b. Through your own knowledge and observations about current events and people.

5. Application to Life and Work – Reflect on application of knowledge about the Early Adulthood stage; to your own life and work right now.
    a. How does knowledge of this stage fit your own life now?
    b. How does knowledge of this stage fit with the work that you do or that you plan to do?

c. How does knowledge of this stage fit with the significant other people in your life – family, best friends, co-workers, life partners, etc?

Case Study with Integration of Kohlberg's Theory

This is a case study of an individual in the early adulthood life-span stage. JE is a 34 year old Caucasian male. He lives alone. He has never been married. He is beginning Bible college this fall. He is a very depended upon staff member of one of the largest, most active churches in America.

Application of Kohlberg's Theory

JE fits within the universal ethical principles of Kohlberg's theory. This is the sixth and highest stage in Kohlberg's theory of moral development. It states by this stage the person has developed a moral standard based on universal human rights. When the person is faced with a conflict between law and conscience, the person will follow conscience, even though the decision might involve personal risk. JE fits within this stage as he will weigh out all factors, but will always go with his conscience no matter the risk to him or the ones he loves.

Cognitive Development

JE is extremely intelligent and will soon be furthering his education. He has a musical mind and borders on genius with these abilities. That keeps his mind working constantly, whether he is actually on the job or not.

Physical Development

JE is the healthiest he has been in his adult life. He is conscious of what he eats and works out regularly, not for physical appearance alone, rather to be healthy. He meets with a nutritionist monthly.

Emotional Development

JE is an overall happy person and tends to always brighten a room. He has a very loud, boisterous personality. He does not let people in to his world easily and does not share of his emotion freely. It takes a lot to break down the walls he has built up around his personal life. He was raised in a divorced home and witnessed a lot as a young child watching his parents go through their divorce. As an adult he has a relationship with his father, but it is far from a father/son relationship. He has a wonderful relationship with his step-father.

Social Development

Even though JE does have walls built around himself, he is rather social. He has a lot of friends and interacts well with others. He never meets a stranger and is kind to all. He brings out the best in those around him. Everyone loves him and thinks he is hilarious. He handles conflict head on and is not afraid to speak his mind.

Moral Development

JE starts Bible college in the fall, his moral compass is strong. He always strives to do the right thing, while following his heart. He knows there is a difference in right and wrong and believes you should always do right by those around you.

Conclusion

In conclusion, JE is on average compared to his life stage with his cognitive skills, social skills, moral development and physical development. His emotional development has room to improve, but is definitely within the realm of a hopeful, positive outcome.

Practice Test Items

1. List and describe six different adult lifestyles.

2. Describe how these key features of early adulthood are demonstrated.
    a. Identity exploration
    b. Instability
    c. Self-focused
    d. Feeling in-between
    e. An age of possibility

3. Describe changes in self-care that can occur with entrance into early adulthood.

4. Describe the role of work with entrance into early adulthood.

5. Discuss these aspects of Attraction in early adulthood
    a. First Impression.
    b. Familiarity and Similarity

c. Physical Attractiveness

Additional Resources

Textbooks

Santrock, J. (2015). *Life-span development.* (15th ed.). Boston: McGraw-Hill Publishers. NOTE: McGraw-Hill also offers an online resource to accompany this text- *Connect.*

Sigelman, C.K. & Rider, E.A. (2014). *Life-span human development* (8th ed.). Belmont, CA: Wadsworth Cengage Learning.

Web Links

https://www.youtube.com/watch?v=l00jK5A9RUU

https://www.youtube.com/watch?v=8NaHepAgoSg

http://psychcentral.com/blog/archives/2012/01/08/7-research-based-principles-for-making-marriage-work/

http://www.letsmakeaplan.org/learning-center/advice-elements-of-a-financial-plan-putting-the-pieces-together/article/lets-make-a-plan-blogs/plan-for-your-future-tips-for-young-professionals

https://www.boundless.com/psychology/textbooks/boundless-psychology-textbook/human-development-14/early-and-middle-adulthood-74/cognitive-development-in-adulthood-288-12823/

Tips for Instructors

While students may easily learn rote facts about the theories, they can better learn application of the theories to life-span development through opportunities for application. Examples are provided in this chapter and with each chapter on the theories for exam items and assignments that can promote integration of theory to life.

Tips for Students

These theories of life-span development provide core understanding of why we live the way we live. To borrow a concept from health care, understanding involves identification of the evidence. As you apply a theory to your life or the life of someone else, think about what is the evidence that you or the other person is representing that facet of that theory.

Middle Adulthood

Background

This is " the developmental period from approximately 40 to about 60 years of age. It is a time of expanding personal and social involvement and responsibility; of assisting the next generation in becoming competent, mature individuals; and of reaching and maintaining satisfaction in a career." (Santrock, 2015, p. 14).

Exercises

1. Journaling – Begin a journal as you study the theories of lifespan development and write reflections about yourself for each theory and stage studied. For the Middle Adulthood stage, describe what you remember about yourself for this stage – you may have to ask parents or other care-givers about that time in your life, but do note any memories that you do have.

2. Observation - Use your journal to take notes from observation of a few people who are currently in the Middle Adulthood stage. As with yourself, note how the person demonstrates what you are learning about that stage.

3. Research – Find a scholarly article on the Middle Adulthood stage of life and summarize that to share with your class. Focus on what the article teaches you about Middle Adulthood and how you can apply that to your life and work.

4. Developmental Problems – Discuss developmental problems that you have learned about with the Middle Adulthood stage of life.
   a. Through some research about this.
   b. Through your own knowledge and observations about current events and people.

5. Application to Life and Work – Reflect on application of knowledge about the Middle Adulthood stage to your own life and work right now.
   a. How does knowledge of this stage fit your own life now?
   b. How does knowledge of this stage fit with the work that you do or that you plan to do?

c. How does knowledge of this stage fit with the significant other people in your life – family, best friends, co-workers, life partners, etc?

Case Study with Integration of Kohlberg's Theory

This is a case study of an individual in the middle adulthood. MH is a 45 year old male Caucasian. He is married and lives in a single family home with two children. He has recently completed his four year BS degree and is currently working full time as a Recreational Specialist.

Application of Kohlberg's Theory

MH fits very closely in stage 6 of Kohlberg's Theory. This post-conventional level teeters on obeying laws and recognizing that an individual's perspective can take precedence over the law (Santrock, 2015, p. 312). Though MH is a rule follower by nature, if he feels passionately about something that would break the rules, he will break the rules. This especially comes into play when it comes to the safety of his family. This way of thinking has probably been reinforced through his discipline in the military.

Cognitive Development

MH has reached the peak of his cognitive development and is actually on the decline. Presently he has found that he has a much harder time remembering recent events and tasks that need accomplished. His long term memory hasn't changed but he has trouble remembering recent past events as well as names. MH doesn't work on his cognitive building specifically but finds that using acronyms when he knows he needs to remember something specific helps. He keeps up with current events by reading the news and watches news programs.

Physical Development

In 2004, MH broke his back while parachuting out of a plane in the US Navy. He worked hard to rebuild his back through strength conditioning and healthy eating habits. He did well keeping his back muscles strong which helped support his back until 2010. In 2010, MH started working on his college degree in an online program. It took a lot of his time that he had once dedicated to working out. His back started deteriorating and he now has chronic pain. Because of this he also has trouble sleeping. He still eats healthy and exercises on a limited basis. He looks to be healthy but often masks the pain with ibuprofen.

Emotional Development

In the last few years, MH has become more anxious about growing older. His deteriorating health and the passing of siblings and parents has caused him to take a long look at his mortality. Though generally a happy person, these issues weigh on him but he typically holds his feelings inside so as not to worry his children. He will talk about it limitedly and it is apparent in his demeanor but he will not discuss it openly.

Social Development

Socially he seems to be a butterfly. Everyone who knows him loves him. He doesn't know a stranger and will talk at lengths to anyone. When he strikes up a conversation, he always focuses on the other person's interests and needs. This is an endearing quality, but inwardly he detests talking to people. He will refuse to do normal tasks like go to the local grocery store for fear of running into someone he knows. He often describes insecurities about talking to people though he never seems to be lacking confidence in a conversation. He states that his faltering memory of people's names and lack of knowing what to talk about gives him anxiety in social settings. He often avoids and dislikes any social setting and is most comfortable and happy at home or with his immediate family only.

Moral Development

MH mostly practices in stage five of Kohlberg's Theory. He is adamant about making the life for his children easier than his own but is frustrated by laws that are made that he feels will hinder them. He is further frustrated because he feels many of these decisions are out of his control. This frustration pushes him into the realm of stage six. He definitely runs into a relative view of morality and is very methodical and justifies his stance if it is outside of the realm of normal rules and regulations if it goes against the grain.

Conclusion

MH is below average in the physical developmental areas, having suffered from several injuries. These injuries have caused a ripple effect of emotional and physical problems causing him to have a below average sleeping pattern, which has resulted in memory issues causing anxiety in social settings. Morally he is higher than most reaching the post-conventional 6th stage of Kohlberg's Theory.

Practice Test Items

1. What are some of the key factors in changing midlife for an adult?
2. Discuss considerations of health, disease, stress and personal control for someone in Middle Adulthood.
3. Describe the difference between Fluid and Crystallized Intelligence
4. Describe the role of leisure for someone in Middle Adulthood.
5. Describe Intergenerational Relationships that often affect persons in Middle Adulthood.

Additional Resources

Textbooks

Santrock, J. (2015). *Life-span development.* (15th ed.). Boston: McGraw-Hill Publishers. NOTE: McGraw-Hill also offers an online resource to accompany this text- *Connect.*

Sigelman, C.K. & Rider, E.A. (2014). *Life-span human development* (8th ed.). Belmont, CA: Wadsworth Cengage Learning.

Web Links

http://healthymidlife.com/

https://www.youtube.com/watch?v=TZZlIKXcolo

http://www.ncbi.nlm.nih.gov/pmc/articles/PMC3915431/.

http://www.helpguide.org/articles/exercise-fitness/exercise-and-fitness-as-you-age.htm

http://www.apa.org/monitor/2011/04/mind-midlife.aspx

Tips for Instructors

While students may easily learn rote facts about the theories, they can better learn application of the theories to life-span development through opportunities for application. Examples are provided in this chapter and with each chapter on the theories for exam items and assignments that can promote integration of theory to life.

Tips for Students

These theories of life-span development provide core understanding of why we live the way we live. To borrow a concept from health care, understanding involves identification of the evidence. As you apply a theory to your life or the life of someone else, think about what is the evidence that you or the other person is representing that facet of that theory.

Late Adulthood

Background

This is the "developmental period that begins during the sixties or seventies and lasts until death. It is a time of life review, retirement, and adjustment to new social roles and diminishing strength and health." (Santrock, 2015, p. 14).

Exercises

1. Journaling – Begin a journal as you study the theories of lifespan development and write reflections about yourself for each theory and stage studied. For the Late Adulthood stage, describe what you remember about yourself for this stage – you may have to ask parents or other care-givers about that time in your life, but do note any memories that you do have.

2. Observation - Use your journal to take notes from observation of a few people who are currently in the Late Adulthood stage. As with yourself, note how the person demonstrates what you are learning about that stage.

3. Research – Find a scholarly article on the Late Adulthood stage of life and summarize that to share with your class. Focus on what the article teaches you about Late Adulthood and how you can apply that to your life and work.

4. Developmental Problems – Discuss developmental problems that you have learned about with the Late Adulthood stage of life.
   a. Through some research about this.
   b. Through your own knowledge and observations about current events and people.

5. Application to Life and Work – Reflect on application of knowledge about the Late Adulthood stage; to your own life and work right now.
   a. How does knowledge of this stage fit your own life now?
   b. How does knowledge of this stage fit with the work that you do or that you plan to do?
   c. How does knowledge of this stage fit with the significant other people in your life – family, best friends, co-workers, life partners, etc?

Case Study

This is a case study of an individual in the late adulthood life-span stage. AR is a 60 year old African American female who lives with her daughter, granddaughter, and grandson. She is an individual who does not have a high school education and only completed up to grade 8. Due to the battle of depression, AR seeks services from Pine Belt, which is a mental health center, and does not hold a job. When most people think of Pine Belt, they think of her having a mental problem, but she attends the facility for her battle with depression only.

Application of the Socioemotional Selectivity Theory

AR has three children and she loves them all equally, but she spends most of her time with her youngest daughter who still lives with her. Her youngest daughter always makes her laughs, allows her to travel with her a lot, and is always showering her with gifts and cash just because. AR does not deliberately surround herself around her youngest daughter because of handouts but because her youngest daughter knows firsthand about the struggles and has always been there to help her. The other children do not do as much as the younger child to ensure that their mother is well taken care of, but they are the ones who she has done the most for.

Cognitive Development

As stated above, AR receives counseling services from a mental health center due to traumatic experiences. Cognitively, she is a very smart individual being that she did not obtain the proper education. She reads a lot and explores the web on her tablet to gain information and insight on certain things. She enjoys playing the game Candy Crush and completing crossword puzzles. She is always up for gaining new information and enjoys listening to her daughters, who are both teachers, discuss different topics they have learned while obtaining their degrees.

Physical Development

AR is 5'7" tall and weighs approximately 215 pounds. She is considered to have a 33.7 BMI that classifies her as obese, according to a body mass index (National Institutes of Health). She is not active at all anymore due to other health problems that she claims limits her ability to exercise. She recently exercised via a workout video at home completing four miles a day. She lost a large amount of weight but began to get out of routine and gained majority of the weight back. AR rarely eats healthy. She enjoys eating fried foods rather than baked foods and all of the other unhealthy choices. AR normally goes to bed at around 12am-1am and sleeps to around 9am.

Emotional Development

At a young age, AR and her husband divorced, she was depressed and was just a total mess. She had two kids and did not know how she would raise them alone; however, she survived. This is when AR began to get services from Pine Belt. Years later, she met her longtime boyfriend who physically and verbally abused her at times, and they eventually parted ways. She immediately slipped into the depression state again because she now had a third child. Her last child got a job and helped her mom out, and they survived. About 3 years ago, AR's mother passed away so that of course took a toll on her. She did not cope well with the death, but with therapy sessions, she conquered that tragedy as well. AR is now a more happy and vibrant person. She generally expresses her emotions by crying and writing about it.

Social Development

Socially, AR interacts well with others. She is normally in the presence of her immediate family. She enjoys interacting on Facebook and reaching out to her old classmates and even some of her relatives. She does not meet any strangers and is an easy person to talk and get along with. She enjoys bonding and spending time with her family the most and will do anything and everything in her power to make that happen every Sunday for a family dinner.

Moral Development

AR was raised back when the older generation did not allow certain things that happen in the new generation. AR was raised in a household where when adults visited her mother, the children automatically knew they were to be outdoors playing. AR also believes in disciplining children by corporal punishment instead of some of the methods individuals use today such as timeout. AR treats everyone with respect, and she refers to her elders as ma'am and sir. She also came from a household where you had to work. They worked in the field as children; so, she raised her children in a way so that they would understand that nothing is given to them. She firmly believes in home cooked meals instead of eating fast foods. She believes in sharing with others as well. For example, AR lives in a community where everyone is mostly related. When she receives different vegetables in abundance such as corn, okra, peas, and etc., she does not keep it all for herself. Instead, she shares it with her neighborhood because she is genuinely a free hearted person.

Conclusion

AR is an individual who does extremely well in many areas, but not so well in others. She reflects back on her life, her health is not as good as she would like for it to be, and she is adjusting well to social interactions. She is on target morally. She knows that you are to always do what is right and not only does she encourage it upon others, but she practices it as well. AR seems to excel when it comes to social interactions. Even though she is getting older, she is able to keep up with the new devices and is quite technology savvy. Older individuals normally refrain from using technology because they just do not know how, or they are afraid that they will do something to harm the device all because they are not familiar with it. Cognitively, AR seems to excel. Due to her lack of education, she is extremely knowledgeable about many things. A person would think she have gone to college because of the significant amount of education she has about different topics. AR is below average when it comes to her physical health and emotional development. If she does not do something physically, she will continue to become larger and larger in size, and it will begin to cause other health problems. Emotionally, AR is improving but has not quite met her goal of how she copes with certain things that have happened in her life. She can sometime have a negative outlook on certain things and can be biased in certain situations all because of her experiences. She sometimes thinks there is nothing any different than the things she has endured. In conclusion, AR is an amazing individual but just as everyone else regardless of age, she still has room to grow and develop.

Practice Test Items

1. Discuss the concept of use It or lose It as applied to Late Adulthood.

2. Discuss some considerations that a person has in adjustment to retirement.

3. Discuss issues that face older adults in their treatment by society.

4. Discuss three areas of strength that centenarians have.

5. Discuss the role of money and finances in the life of someone in Late Adulthood.

Additional Resources

Textbooks

Santrock, J. (2015). *Life-span development*. (15th ed.). Boston: McGraw-Hill Publishers. NOTE: McGraw-Hill also offers an online resource to accompany this text- *Connect.*

Sigelman, C.K. & Rider, E.A. (2014). *Life-span human development* (8th ed.). Belmont, CA: Wadsworth Cengage Learning.

Web Links

http://www.alz.org/index.asp

https://www.youtube.com/watch?v=5MLL288Gr6o

https://www.ivcc.edu/uploadedFiles/_faculty/_mangold/Chapter%2024%20%20Late%20Adulthood%20Cognitive%20Development.pdf

https://www.ncpc.org/resources/files/pdf/violent-crime/older_americans_2.pdf

https://www.ncoa.org/audience/older-adults-caregivers-resources/

Tips for Instructors

While students may easily learn rote facts about the theories, they can better learn application of the theories to life-span development through opportunities for application. Examples are provided in this chapter and with each chapter on the theories for exam items and assignments that can promote integration of theory to life.

Tips for Students

These theories of life-span development provide core understanding of why we live the way we live. To borrow a concept from health care, understanding involves identification of the evidence. As you apply a theory to your life or the life of someone else, think about what is the evidence that you or the other person is representing that facet of that theory.

Endings

Background

As there is a beginning to life during the prenatal period of development, life also has an ending in the event of death of a person. This chapter focuses on aspects of that event that the person may experience and that those connected to the person may also experience as this individual dies.

Exercises

1. Journaling – Begin a journal as you study the theories of lifespan development and write reflections about yourself for each theory and stage studied. For the Endings stage, describe any experiences that you have had with someone in this stage of life.

2. Observation - Use your journal to take notes from observation of a few people who are currently in the Endings stage – either through the process of a terminal illness, time as a hospice patient, or in a period of grief over the loss of someone else. As with yourself, note how the person demonstrates what you are learning about that stage.

3. Research – Find a scholarly article on the Endings stage of life and summarize that to share with your class. Focus on what the article teaches you about Endings and how you can apply that to your life and work.

4. Developmental Problems – Discuss developmental problems that you have learned about with the Endings stage of life.
    a. Through some research about this.
    b. Through your own knowledge and observations about current events and people.

5. Application to Life and Work – Reflect on application of knowledge about the Endings stage; to your own life and work right now.
    a. How does knowledge of this stage fit your own life now?
    b. How does knowledge of this stage fit with the work that you do or that you plan to do?
    c. How does knowledge of this stage fit with the significant other people in your life – family, best friends, co-workers, life partners, etc?

Case Study

This website describes the thoughts and feelings that accompany someone who is going through the stages of the Kubler-Ross model of grief and dying.

http://www.drchristinahibbert.com/dealing-with-grief/5-stages-of-grief/

Practice Test Items

1. Compare these components of the death system in two different cultures.

   a. Places or Contexts
   b. Symbols
   c. Times
   d. Objects
   e. People

2. Describe the general attitudes and perceptions of death across these life-span stages.

   a. Childhood
   b. Adolescence
   c. Early Adulthood
   d. Middle Adulthood
   e. Late Adulthood

Additional Resources

Textbooks

Santrock, J. (2015). *Life-span development*. (15th ed.). Boston: McGraw-Hill Publishers. NOTE: McGraw-Hill also offers an online resource to accompany this text- *Connect.*

Sigelman, C.K. & Rider, E.A. (2014). *Life-span human development* (8th ed.). Belmont, CA: Wadsworth Cengage Learning.

Woolfolk, A. & Perry, N.E. (2015). *Child and Adolescent Development* (2nd ed.). Upper Saddle River, NJ: Pearson.

Web Links

http://www.helpstartshere.org/health-and-wellness/death-and-dying/death-and-dying-resources.html

http://www.growthhouse.org/

http://www.ekrfoundation.org/five-stages-of-grief/

http://www.cancer.net/coping-with-cancer/managing-emotions/grief-and-loss/understanding-grief-within-cultural-context

http://www.nmha.org/conditions/coping-loss-bereavement-and-grief

Tips for Instructors

While students may easily learn rote facts about the theories, they can better learn application of the theories to life-span development through opportunities for application. Examples are provided in this chapter and with each chapter on the theories for exam items and assignments that can promote integration of theory to life.

Tips for Students

These theories of life-span development provide core understanding of why we live the way we live. To borrow a concept from health care, understanding involves identification of the evidence. As you apply a theory to your life or the life of someone else, think about what is the evidence that you or the other person is representing that facet of that theory.

Reflection on Personal Development

Background

Study of lifespan development can open the eyes and the insight of a student to his or her own development over the years. It is meaningful for students to reflect back and even compare self during childhood to their current lifespan stage per the discussion of those lifespan stages in their textbook. This section of the workbook provides exercises for students to do this self-reflection and also a template for a self case-study on lifespan development.

Exercises

Complete the Personal Wellness Plan and Questionnaire at the end of this section. This will give you an indication of your developmental status in areas of personal development and is a tool that you can use to monitor yourself periodically.

Case Study

Develop a case study on yourself to include the following sections in either a paper format or a Power Point presentation using the Pecha Kucha format at https://davefoord.wordpress.com/2011/01/18/creating-a-quick-fire-powerpoint-pecha-kucha/

Case Study on Self Content	Slide Number
Introduction and Identifying Information	1-2
Application of two theories to self – student's choice of theories. Each theory should have 3 slides	3-8
Cognitive Development	9 – 10
Physical Development	11-12
Emotional Development	13-14
Social Development	15-16
Moral Development	17-18

Conclusion – what student has learned about his or her own development.	19-20
Presentation Script with 3 references (may include text).	
Recording for PPT	
Total Final Points	

Personal Wellness Questionnaire & Plan

Whether the major focus of your life is being a student, working a job, or enjoying your retirement – there are multiple areas of your life that contribute to the success of your major focus. Those areas together make up your personal wellness.

The purpose of this questionnaire is to indicate your current profile of overall wellness and to help you plan a foundation from which to build and strengthen your different areas of personal wellness – to better support the major focus of your life.

INSTRUCTIONS:

In each of the following 8 components of personal wellness, please indicate how often the following statements apply to you. For the total score for each component, add up the columns and enter the total of those.

Emotional - Having high self-esteem and confidence, satisfying relationships, a support network, and staying optimistic.

Priority for Effort	Statement	Very little of the time – score of 1	Sometimes – score of 2	Most of the time – Score of 3
	I have a well-developed sense of my own attitudes and values.			
	I average 7-8 hours of sleep daily.			
	I find healthy ways to cope with stress (e.g. exercise, relaxation, social support).			

	I am able to cope with feelings of sadness and worry.			
	I seek counseling if I face problematic or enduring emotional difficulties in my life.			
Total Score	Total Score of all three columns:			

Financial - Maintaining a balanced budget for expenses while also practicing money-saving techniques. Preparedness for all expenses, including short-term, long-term, and emergencies.

Priority for Effort	Statement	Very little of the time – score of 1	Sometimes – score of 2	Most of the time – score of 3
	I budget my funds so that I do not run out of money.			
	I balance my checkbook regularly.			
	I know my total amount of debt.			
	I have 1 or no credit cards (debit cards not included).			
	I am never late on payments.			
	I put money into savings on a regular basis.			
	I have at least 10% of my annual income in an interest earning savings account.			
Total Score	Total Score of all three columns:			

Intellectual - Getting the most out of life by asking questions, being open to new ideas, learning new skills, and studying effectively.

Priority for Effort	Statement	Very little of the time – score of 1	Sometimes – score of 2	Most of the time – score of 3
	I look for ways to learn more about a variety of things.			
	I take on challenges as a chance to learn.			
	I am curious about things.			
	I am creative.			
	I try to improve myself.			
	I do something several times a week to work my brain, such as puzzles, studying, or hobbies.			
	I read.			
Total Score	Total Score of all three columns:			

Physical – Maintaining optimal health by getting enough sleep, eating healthy, exercising, and avoiding unhealthy habits.

Priority for Effort	Statement	Very little of the time – score of 1	Sometimes – score of 2	Most of the time – score of 3
	I am active at least 20-30 minutes two to three days a week.			
	I maintain healthy eating patterns.			
	I eat at least 5 servings of fresh fruits and vegetables daily.			

	I drink zero to no more than 1 drink a day (women) or 2 drinks a day (men).			
	I avoid harmful use of drugs (includes tobacco, marijuana, alcohol, etc.).			
	I practice safe sex (e.g. use a condom, partners test negative for STIs) or practice abstinence.			
	I see a health care practitioner if I can't solve a health concern on my own.			
	I manage my weight in healthy ways.			
Total Score	**Total Score of all three columns:**			

Social – Having a supportive social network, contributing to society, and valuing cultural diversity.

Priority for Effort	Statement	Very little of the time – score of 1	Sometimes – score of 2	Most of the time – score of 3
	I am satisfied with my social life.			
	I am involved in at least one group (ie civic club, church, sports team, etc.)			

	I maintain a network of supportive friends/family/ social contacts.			
	I have a least one meaningful relationship.			
	I am accepting of the diversity of others (i.e. race, religion, gender, ability, etc.).			
	I give priority to my own needs by saying "no" to others' request of me when applicable.			
Total Score	**Total Score of all three columns:**			

Spiritual – Possessing a set of guiding beliefs, principles, or values that give meaning and purpose to life, having a clear understanding of right and wrong, seeing the beauty in life and finding joy in everyday life. Spiritual wellness is also the capacity to love, have compassion for others, forgiveness, joy, and fulfillment.

Priority for Effort	Statement	Very little of the time – score of 1	Sometimes – score of 2	Most of the time – score of 3
	I have a belief system (e.g., spiritual, atheist).			
	I have a sense of purpose in my life.			
	I take time for spiritual growth/ development.			
	I utilize resources to improve my well-being.			

	I spend time reflecting and meditating.			
Total Score	Total Score of all three columns:			

Time Management – Managing time smartly to have more time to do the things we want to do.

Priority for Effort	Statement	Very little of the time – score of 1	Sometimes – score of 2	Most of the time – score of 3
	I plan some "me time" each day.			
	I use a prioritized list of "Things to Do".			
	I begin my day with a plan of action.			
	I keep the different areas of my life in balance.			
	I keep my life's "stuff" organized.			
Total Score	Total Score of all three columns:			

Work (paid or unpaid) – The ability to get personal fulfillment from our work while still maintaining balance in our lives. Our desire to contribute to make a positive impact on the organizations we work in and to society as a whole.

Priority for Effort	Statement	Very little of the time – score of 1	Sometimes – score of 2	Most of the time – score of 3
	I spend some time each week doing a job, volunteer or service work, or work at home, such as chores or hobbies.			

	I am developing the necessary skills to achieve my work goals.			
	I have confidence in my skills to do the work I want.			
	I work effectively with others.			
	I know where to find work to do that I am interested in doing.			
Total Score	**Total Score of all three columns:**			

Culture – growth and functioning within "shared values, beliefs, expectations, worldview, symbols, and appropriate learned behaviors of a group that provide its members with norms, plans, traditions, and rules for social living." (Gladding, 2011, p. 44)

Gladding, s. (2011). *The counseling dictionary: Concise definitions of frequently used terms* (3rd. ed). Upper Saddle River, N.J: Merrill.

Priority for Effort	Statement	Very little of the time – score of 1	Sometimes – score of 2	Most of the time – score of 3
	I have a group to whom I belong that fits the definition above of culture.			
	I live in a setting such as a neighborhood, apartment complex, or community with others a culture that I identify with.			
	I share values and a worldview with those whom I consider to be of the same culture that I identify with			

	I follow practices that are representative of my culture, such as my dress, my religious practices, and my observation of holidays.			
	I consider my personal value and belief system to represent that of my culture.			
Total Score	**Total Score of all three columns:**			

TOTAL WELLNESS SCORE: Add up your scores for all 9 components of wellness to give you your total wellness score.

PRIORITY FOR EFFORT: It is common for people to have some areas in which they are well much of the time, some areas in which they are well some of the time, and some areas in which they are well very little or none of the time. As you look back at your scores in the different areas, note the areas in which you indicated "very little of the time." Pick one of these in each of the 8 wellness components to prioritize your efforts for improvement. If you were well enough in a component that your lowest scores were "sometimes," then choose one of these response areas as a priority for attention.

NOW you are ready to develop your Personal Wellness Plan.

FOLLOW-UP PLAN: Complete the following for each priority area that you indicated.

Area to work on:____

Things I can to do make this improvement.	When will you start doing this?	How often will you do this?	What resources do you need to get to help you this (money, people, etc)?

NOW – GO DO IT!

To keep yourself on track, review the questionnaire on a regular basis (such as monthly or quarterly) to check if you have made improvement or gone backwards in areas. Becoming well and staying well requires regular maintenance – just like our vehicles. A regular check-up can help you stay well better and help you better accomplish the main focus of your life.

Conclusion on Application to Professional and Personal Life

While many degree programs require a course in lifespan development, this course can be extremely useful beyond just the credit hours for degree completion. This last section of the workbook provides a few ideas for students to apply the workbook and course textbook contents to their own careers as well as work with other people in a personal modality such as with family or community work.

1. Use the life expectancy survey at one or both of the following sites to get an idea of how your current lifestyle will affect the length and quality of your life.

https://www.myabaris.com/tools/life-expectancy-calculator-how-long-will-i-live/

http://www.mccc.edu/~jenningh/Courses/documents/Handout-LifeExpectancySurvey.pdf

After completing the survey, write down actions that you can take to improve your longevity and quality of life.

2. Use the same survey in number 1 above to share with others to help them increase their own longevity and quality of life.

3. Life is made up of challenges and successes. Whatever work you do and with your family and friends, encourage them to periodically take time to stop on reflect on:

   a. What has been my life in the past?
   b. What is my life now?
   c. What do I want my life to be in the future?

It is through this periodic self-reflection on their life journey that people can gain the insight on what to keep and what to change.

4. Take these phrases about life and periodically reflect on them for yourself or share these with family, friends, co-workers, and students. In your own reflection, consider how these relate to your study about the life-span during this course.

a. I don't want to earn my living; I want to live.-***Oscar Wilde***
b. Live and Let Live – Scottish Proverb
c. Work hard. Dream big.-***Unknown***
d. Life is short. Live passionately.-***Unknown***
e. Life shrinks or expands in proportion to one's courage.-*Anais Nin*
f. Life is a one time offer, use it well.-***Unknown***
g. Life must be lived forwards, but can only be understood backwards.-*Kierkegaard*
h. The trouble is you think you have time.- *Buddha*
i. Whatever you are, be a good one.-*Abraham Lincoln*
j. Be the change you wish to see in the world.-*Unknown*
k. Life is ten percent what happens to you and ninety percent how you respond to it.-*Lou Holtz*
l. Love the life you live, and live the life you love.-*Bob Marley*
m. Live each day as if it's your last.-*Unknown*
n. Life is a mirror and will reflect back to the thinker what he thinks into it.-*Ernest Holmes*
o. The key to immortality is first living a life worth remembering.-*Bruce Lee*

Case Study

Think of someone you would like to understand better, such as on someone you work with, teach, or a family member Using the same format that you used for a case study on yourself, write a case study on that person. Doing this will help you to better understand the developmental factors that have brought them to be the people that they are now.

References

Corey, G. (2013). *Theory and practice of counseling and psychotherapy (9th ed.)* Belmont, CA: Brooks/Cole Cengage Learning

Gladding, s. (2011). *The counseling dictionary: Concise definitions of frequently used terms* (3rd. ed). Upper Saddle River, N.J: Merrill.

Santrock, J. (2015). *Life-span development.* (15th ed.). Boston: McGraw-Hill Publishers. NOTE: McGraw-Hill also offers an online resource to accompany this text- *Connect.*

Sigelman, C.K. & Rider, E.A. (2014). *Life-span human development* (8th ed.). Belmont, CA: Wadsworth Cengage Learning.

Woolfork, A. & Perry, N. (2015). *Child and adolescent development* (2nd ed.) Upper Saddle River, NJ: Pearson.

Abut the Author

The author, Mary Ann Hollingsworth holds her PhD in Counseling Psychology and Health Psychology. She has sixteen years of experience as a counselor in educational as well as community settings and with individuals, families, and groups from Early Childhood to Late Adulthood. In addition, she has 20 years experience as an officer of the United States Army, and 10 years of experience teaching in higher education. She currently teaches students preparing to be school and community mental health counselors.